Alternative Investments Technology

The alternative investments technology market is still considered young and highly diverse, driving varied technology needs. Few players can address the needs of the entire market, while new specialized providers continue to emerge, making choices even more complex. Investors now demand more rigorous due diligence, greater access to senior management, and more detailed, frequent data reports before committing to funds. In response, firms must be agile, ready to reassess, and revamp their operations and practices.

Alternative Investments Technology: Bridging the Gap is tailored for investment professionals, managers, and technologists navigating this evolving landscape. It explores how technology enhances management and investment processes, helping firms maintain competitive advantage and operational efficiency. The book provides insights into leveraging technology for better decision-making, improved efficiency, and enhanced investor outcomes. As technology integration in alternative investments evolves, staying informed is essential. This book serves as an indispensable guide to thriving in this dynamic environment.

Alternative Investments Technology

Bridging the Gap

Ankur Agarwal

CRC Press
Taylor & Francis Group
Boca Raton London New York

CRC Press is an imprint of the
Taylor & Francis Group, an **informa** business

AN AUERBACH BOOK

Cover: Web Large Image (Public)

First edition published 2025
2385 NW Executive Center Drive, Suite 320, Boca Raton FL 33431

and by CRC Press
4 Park Square, Milton Park, Abingdon, Oxon, OX14 4RN

CRC Press is an imprint of Taylor & Francis Group, LLC

© 2025 Taylor & Francis Group, LLC

ISBN: 9781032763880 (hbk)
ISBN: 9781032771786 (pbk)
ISBN: 9781003481652 (ebk)

DOI: 10.1201/9781003481652

Typeset in Garamond
by Newgen Publishing UK

Contents

Preface

Author's Note: In the course of writing this Preface, ChatGPT-4, an advanced AI language model developed by OpenAI, was utilized minimally only to edit, paraphrase and improve clarity where the content has to be presented in a concise manner.

The alternative investments technology services market is still considered young. As it has been growing, so have the software services made available by the service providers. The clients these service providers serve are in an industry that is far from homogeneous. Fund managers vary widely in size, focus, and structure. This diversity drives much of the technology needs and thus there are very few players that can meet the needs of the entire market. New service providers keep coming onto the market (targeting specific specialized segment) thus making the choices even more complex. On top of that, investors are now demanding more rigorous due diligence on both front- and back-office operations, greater access to senior management, and more detailed and frequent data reports before committing to funds. Additionally, regulations such as the Alternative Investment Fund Managers Directive (AIFMD) in Europe and the Dodd-Frank Act in the United States keep on increasing level of regulatory scrutiny from bodies like the U.S. Securities and Exchange Commission (SEC).

In response, alternative investment firms must be agile – ready to reassess and potentially revamp their established business practices, operations, and functions. Questions that firms need to consider include whether their business processes are streamlined enough, if information flow between internal and external stakeholders is effective, and how they can enhance their business to thrive in a dynamic global market. Addressing these questions requires a clear vision for the future and a continuous process of implementing this vision through efficient, flexible, and sustainable business models and processes. In this transformative process, technology plays an essential role, enabling firms to adapt and respond effectively to the rapidly evolving market conditions.

This book is tailored for investment professionals, managers, and technologists who are navigating the rapidly evolving technological landscape of the alternative investment sector. The purpose of this book is not to teach the fundamentals of alternative investments themselves but to explore how technology is used to enhance their management and investment processes. As technology becomes a critical factor in maintaining competitive advantage and operational efficiency, understanding its application and impact is essential for anyone involved in this sector.

Chapter 1 provides an overview of the core and operational functions within alternative investments, setting the stage for a deeper understanding of where and how technology can be integrated. This foundation is crucial for grasping the more complex discussions that follow, as each subsequent chapter builds on this knowledge.

In Chapter 2, we examine the global market of alternative investments through a technological lens, identifying key players and detailing how technology influences their roles and interactions. This global perspective highlights the integration of technology in facilitating smoother, faster, and more secure transactions and interactions across borders.

The discussion then shifts in Chapter 3 to the specific technologies shaping alternative investments today. Here, we define essential systems and terminologies, map out the technological landscape, and discuss the critical challenges that firms face in adapting to new technologies. This chapter serves as a primer for the more detailed exploration of specific technology dilemmas encountered by investment professionals.

Chapters 4 through 9 address these dilemmas, each focused on a particular aspect of technology management within alternative investments. From deciding what processes to automate in Chapter 4 to choosing the right technological solutions in Chapter 5 and determining the optimal infrastructure for running these systems in Chapter 6, each chapter tackles a significant challenge. Further discussions include weighing the costs and benefits of automation, ensuring secure access to systems, and strategically approaching technology transformation. These chapters provide a toolkit for making informed decisions that align technology strategy with business objectives.

Finally, Chapter 10 projects into the future, examining emerging technology trends such as artificial intelligence, blockchain, and cloud computing, and their potential impacts on the alternative investments industry. This foresight is vital for staying ahead of the curve in a rapidly changing digital landscape.

This book aims to bridge the gap between technology and alternative investment management, providing readers with insights into leveraging technology for better decision-making, enhanced efficiency, and improved investor outcomes. Whether you are directly involved in the management of alternative investments or you provide technological support to those who are, the discussions herein will enhance your understanding and strategic application of technology in this complex field.

While the technology integration in alternative investments is still evolving, learning more about it and keeping up with these changes is a must. I trust this book will be your aide through the technological maze of alternative investment management, where it will provide you with the needed skills and knowledge to succeed in this dynamic environment.

Author

Ankur Agarwal has worked in the technology sector for nearly 24 years and is currently the co-founder and chief technology officer at PE Front Office. Previously, Ankur was the Enterprise Architect with Actis, a private equity firm with a focus on emerging markets, where he was responsible for the technology arm of all the business systems of the firm. At Actis, Ankur played a key role in defining and owning business systems landscape and delivery including off-the-shelf and bespoke solutions from both technical and functional perspective.

Prior to this, Ankur was at Sapient Corporation (now Publicis Sapient), a consulting company providing business, marketing, and technology services to the clients, and worked as a lead program architect on several large engagements for clients in various business domains like insurance, travel, media, and telecom.

Ankur has employed his leadership skills and technology expertise to define, design, and implement many large and complex business solutions internationally, across many sectors and, for last 15 years, has been focused on alternative investments technology. During his career he has worked with organizations such as Lloyds of London, Hilton Hotels, General Motors, Avis, News International, Ares Asia, PAG, Edelweiss Alternatives, SIDBI, Sanari Capital, Chiratae Ventures, Samara Capital, 27four Investment Managers, SC Lowy, Silverdale Group, and RMB Ventures.

Chapter 1

Overview of Alternative Investments

1.1 Introduction

It's not straightforward to define alternative investments since they represent the investment options that fall outside the conventional or traditional categories of stocks, bond, and cash. Alternative investments encompass a range of assets, including real estate, commodities, hedge funds, private equity, venture capital (VC), private debt, and fund of funds (FoFs), among others. The alternative assets industry has recorded immense growth in recent years – it is becoming bigger in terms of fund sizes and is also becoming increasingly global with increased interests in emerging markets. Whereas this book does not intend to explain the business concepts of alternative investments or how these asset classes work, it does provide some essential context for the subject of transforming alternative investment firms through advances in information technology (IT). In this book focus will be on a subset of

DOI: 10.1201/9781003481652-1

alternative investments that have increasingly become integral to investors' portfolios, that is, private equity, VC, private debt, and FoFs. To be able to understand the wider landscape, the unique challenges of larger fund sizes, the impact of alternative assets globalizing nature and how technology is a positive influence, the first two chapters will touch on the various high-level aspects of alternative investments structure along with the stakeholders involved in their respective functions. These two chapters will focus on setting up the context for the remaining chapters, which are dedicated to how to apply a method to determine technology needs for an alternative investment firm and then provides detailed guidance on several dilemmas faced by the decision-makers when evaluating various technology systems as well as when making choices.

1.2 Business Model of Alternative Investments – How Does It Work?

For all the asset classes of alternative investments the business model is fundamentally about capital allocation in non-traditional assets that are not publicly traded with the intent to generate higher returns than market indices. Private capital is deployed via different strategies (asset classes) however, in the context of this book, some of them are: private equity, VC, private debt, and FoFs. Irrespective of the strategy these funds are organized using a limited partner/general partner (LP/GP) structure and involve three main stakeholder "groups" – the investors, the alternative investment firms, and the companies in which investment is made. Within each group there are multiple stakeholders aligned to the common objective (of their respective groups) in the whole investment cycle. Though each alternative investment firm may have a different investment strategy, different sector (industry) and regional focus and different fund sizes, their objectives, high-level operating model, and stakeholders remain the same to a good extent. Figure 1.1 shows how different stakeholder groups are involved in the high-level alternative investment business model.

As illustrated in Figure 1.1, capital for an alternative investment fund is sourced from institutional investors, such as major pension funds or financial institutions, insurance entities, affluent individuals or families, and the partners within the firm itself. These contributors are commonly consolidated into a collective investment vehicle and are structurally designated as LPs. Prior to solidifying an investment, multiple parties within an LP interact with counterparts from the fund manager's office. Within an LP, for instance, there exist departments responsible for carrying out tasks such as analytical assessment and operational due diligence of the fund manager. Recently, LPs have been placing a heightened emphasis on the valuation, adherence to regulatory compliance, and the scrutiny of operational risks associated with back-office functions during their due diligence of fund managers. Consequently, for the fund manager, maintaining data management systems that are not only accurate and secure but also in compliance with policy and efficiency standards is critical to shape investor perception during the operational due diligence phase.

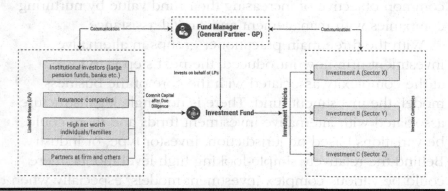

Figure 1.1   Business Model of Alternative Investments.

The fund manager or GP shown in Figure 1.1 manages the day-to-day operations of the alternative investment firm. The GP makes the investments on behalf of the LPs, and in the process involves multiple stakeholders. For example, internal research teams and intermediaries are involved in sourcing deals, then the analyst team gathers information and runs analysis, and the investment committee advises on the investment. These functions require not only access to external information databases but also the internal ability to capture, process, analyze and present before a decision can be made. Similarly, another stakeholder in alternative investment firms is the investor relations team which competes for investors' capital by developing a comprehensive business strategy and demonstrating a solid track record of successful investments. Hence, at the least, these stakeholders need some mechanism or systems that can help them extract and report, current as well as past information about the relevant fund's performance.

The way the GP and the portfolio company stakeholders interact is governed by the level of operational influence that the alternative investment firm can exert on their portfolio companies, which could range from providing the capital to work actively for creating to enhancing the value of the portfolio company. Each alternative investment firm differs in terms of its resources and strategies. However, they share a common objective of increasing their fund value by nurturing companies with management and capital assistance.

With the three main practitioner groups in alternative investment firm now introduced, the next step is to look at the complexity associated with the core of the business model: the investment fund. There is no single legal structure associated with alternative investment funds and there could be variations based on jurisdiction, investor type, or industry. Behind the relatively simple-looking high-level model, there could be various complex investment models, especially when investment is made through an investment vehicle such as some form of special purpose vehicle (SPV). Figure 1.2 shows a few possible scenarios of investment through various types of investment vehicles.

Figure 1.2 introduces a quartet of investment structures, beginning in the top left and proceeding clockwise. The initial setup presents a situation where all investors, co-investors included, channel their funds into a target company via a singular investment vehicle or SPV. In this arrangement, all the investing funds will share the same securities issued by the SPV (shareholder loan, equity). The subsequent arrangement showcases a structure where diverse funds inject capital into the target entity through distinct SPVs, resulting in each fund holding a unique set of SPV securities. The third setup unfolds a scenario in which the GP entity disburses investments in the target through a multitude of SPVs, leading to a single fund possessing various SPV securities connected to the same

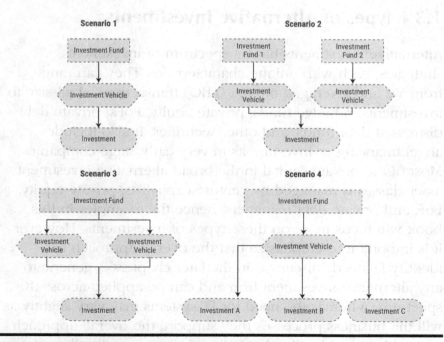

Figure 1.2   Alternative Investment Scenarios.

investment. The final arrangement depicts a private equity firm deploying the same SPV for a series of investments, with the SPV housing multiple securities, each representative of the different investee companies.

The illustration of these four investment scenarios in Figure 1.2 is aimed at unraveling the intricate and distinct features inherent in each investment model. Each approach carries its own set of financial, operational, and technological demands, particularly in terms of accounting, reporting, and IT infrastructure. Given the diversity and potential evolution of investment arrangements within the alternative investment sphere, any operational system in place must be versatile enough to accommodate not only the current complex scenarios but also adapt to future developments to ensure it remains robust over time.

1.3 Types of Alternative Investments

Alternative investments have a spectrum of investment strategies, each with unique characteristics. They can range from VC and leveraged buyout (LBO) transactions of all size to investments in hedge funds, private equity, FoFs, private debt, distressed debt funds, and other securities. It also includes angel financing or investments in very early-stage companies. Most of the private capital in the broad alternative investment asset classes is managed by venture capitalists, private equity, FoF, and private debt managers; hence the examples in this book will focus more on these types of investments. However, it is important to emphasize that the overall approach to identify IT needs discussed in the later chapters is generic to any alternative investment firm and can be applied across the spectrum. Whereas the need for IT systems may vary slightly as will the business processes they support, the overall approach around how to identify, define, build/choose, and rollout the systems will largely be the same. For the asset classes being focused on an alternative asset investment can be made through different investment routes as shown in Figure 1.3.

Figure 1.3 shows the simplest forms of alternative investment means involving the entities – investors (LP), FoFs, investment funds, fund manager (GP), investment vehicles, and investee companies. With legal, tax, and compliance considerations coming into equation, this could become very complex, for example, having onshore and offshore funds in a pari passu structure or master-feeder structure having a multi-feeder structure. Then an investor doing co-investment would need additional handling in the IT systems of the alternative asset firm handling it. Typically, experienced and mature investors could opt for co-investment and direct investments in companies for higher rate of return. Subsequently this co-investment partnership may make numerous "follow-on investments" to the original investment in a different class of securities and/or at different valuation. Thus, having a complex fund structure or allowing the provisions for co-investment would need to take into consideration the additional complexity involved in accounting, reporting, management fee, partnership expenses, transfers, compliance, etc. And thus, with every other means of alternative asset investment there would be some

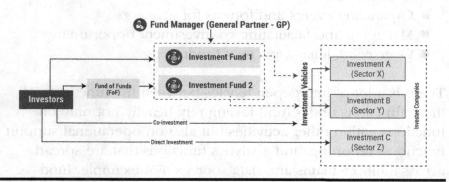

Figure 1.3 Primary Means of Alternative Asset Investment.

changes in the business process and the overall handling from investment till the exit.

1.4 Primary Functions

An alternative investment firm's functions can be classified into core business functions (or investment functions) and operational support functions. Teams across the functions operate with the aim of promoting the profitability of the firm and its investments in their respective areas of influence.

1.4.1 Core Business Functions

The core business "activities" for any alternative investment firm can be broadly classified as – fund raising, making investment, monitor investment, planning divestment, and capital redistribution. These high-level core "activities" involve multiple "functions" within each of them, for example, fund raising activity involves functions like:

- Managing relationships and communications with investors
- Conducting due diligence for fundraising initiatives
- Crafting and distributing fundraising communications, data, and materials
- Organizing events and forums for investors
- Managing and facilitating co-investment opportunities
- Overseeing legal aspects of fundraising

There is a lot of interdependencies between the functions. All these functions under fund raising rely heavily not only on functions within other activities but also on operational support functions, reporting, and analytics functions that are spread across multiple teams and data sources. For example, fund raising materials would include preparation of performance reports of existing investments by investment managers and fund raising communications might involve IT team for sending bulk emails or targeted emails. In Figure 1.4, these core activities have been categorized as front-, middle-, and back-office activities.

Figure 1.4 shows how an alternative investment firm is typically organized operationally, highlighting the interconnectivity of the front, middle, and back office in carrying out the firm's functions effectively. As seen in Figure 1.4, functions like reporting, analytics, and operational support span across the front-, middle-, and back-office activities and work like threads that weave together the units of the firm and make them work cohesively and efficiently. Such functions not only get reused across the activities but also involve processing of information coming from multiple activities and sources. The next section touches upon support function; hence in this section let's see what reporting and analytics entail.

Effective reporting must ensure that information needed by investors, regulators, and the alternative investment firms themselves is served timely and accurately. Whether looking at pipeline or portfolio company or fund, it's critical for alternative

FRONT OFFICE	MIDDLE OFFICE	BACK OFFICE
• Deal Origination & Sourcing	• Investment Monitoring	• Fund Management and Accounting
• Deal Execution & Making Investments	• Performance Analysis	• Capital Redistribution
• Investor Relations	• Risk Management	• Waterfall Calculation
• Fund Raising	• Planning Divestment (Exit)	

(Operational Support Functions along both left and right margins)

Reporting

Analytics (Forecasting, Benchmarking)

Figure 1.4   Activities for an Alternative Investment Firm.

investment firms to draw comparisons and analysis across various companies on desirable parameters to have meaningful real-time assessment of the performance. Slicing and dicing of deal data is important for internal reviews as well as LP reporting. It's essential to be able to have a future-looking view of the investment performance by tweaking certain parameters that can change with time, for example, portfolio's financial data and currency fluctuations. Multi-region and multi-currency reporting capability taking future "what-if" scenarios into consideration is invaluable for any alternative investment firm as it allows operating with greater certainty and caution. Analytics is key to forecasting, benchmarking, and risk analysis and empowers an alternative investment firm to take informed, data-driven decision and mitigate risks that could hamper returns on their invested capital. Reporting and analytics require a robust infrastructure that can source data from multiple sources and process accurately providing insights into performance, trends, and risks. Transparency to investors and compliance (e.g., compliance to International Private Equity and Venture Capital Association (IPEV), Institutional Limited Partners Association (ILPA) "Reporting and Valuation Guidelines") are also highly desirable needs when it comes to alternative investment reporting.

1.4.2 Operational Support Functions

Apart from the core functions every alternative investment firm also need functions to support the organization. Operational functions can be defined as everything else not directly involved with the investment management function of the firm. The "activities" covered within the operational functions of a firm include fund accounting, trade operations, compliance, and IT. These also include functions like human resource (HR), payroll management, corporate finance, staffing, and office administration.

The operational functions are not less important and without the operational support functions the capital allocation and investment functions could not operate. For example, an alternative investment firm requires – transaction accounting and legal tasks for deal completion. Investor communications involve generating correspondence such as letters, faxes, and emails, as well as preparing documents like drawdown instructions and repayment notices. Portfolio management necessitates maintaining a complete income history, comparing expected versus received income by date, amount, and portfolio company, while tracking various income types including interest, dividends, and fees. Human resources functions encompass conducting performance appraisals and planning headcount. The finance department handles tasks such as preparing tax returns. Hence, cross-functional support is crucial, with HR, IT, and finance teams collaborating with or enabling core business teams by providing data and systems to improve operational efficiency. Operational functions may relatively rely more on service providers to be able to best address the needs of investment functions.

By now it's obvious that aforementioned supporting functions are huge enablers for the core business functions and the front-, middle-, and back-office activities would struggle to work efficiently in the absence of strong and technology-enabled supporting functions.

1.5 Summary

Every alternative investment firm, depending on its region and industry focus, may have unique investment, monitoring, and divestment strategies. Core business functions and operational support functions are complementary functions; however, due to these unique strategies each firm may require tailored operations to be able to aptly support investment functions.

This chapter has highlighted complexities embedded in their core business functions due to this uniqueness. For smooth operations in an alternative asset firm, core function should be well augmented with support functions. Utilizing operational support functions permits fund managers to concentrate on the core operations, minimize administrative costs, and ensure data integrity and accuracy. The next chapter will build upon this context and present specifics about alternative investment domain and who does what in a typical private equity, VC, private debt, and FoFs setup.

Chapter 2

Alternative Investments: Global Market

2.1 Introduction

The alternative investment sector has seen remarkable growth worldwide, emerging as a prominent option for investors everywhere. While top alternative investment firms primarily target the European and American markets, they have also made strides in key developing economies like Africa, Brazil, Russia, China, and India. With the industry's expansion comes a soaring demand for information, necessitating a greater number of researchers and specialists who possess an in-depth knowledge of their specific region, sector, and function. Quick and easy access to all kinds of information is essential for these business operations. Alternative investment firms require advanced tools to gather data from different markets, areas, and people to form well-rounded and integrated perspectives that allow for comparison on various levels. Underpinned by such needs and rapid technological and digital advancement, the global alternative investment landscape is undergoing a profound transformation. This chapter will explore the structure and roles of different players in the worldwide alternative investment scene and outline the internal functional setup of a standard alternative investment company or a private capital company to be precise.

2.2 Alternative Investments Market Players

The previous chapter briefly introduced the roles of general partners (GPs) and limited partners (LPs) in alternative investment space. However, it is important to remember that the whole alternative investment market structure is not made up of just LPs and GPs. Institutional investors, hedge funds, private equity firms, venture capitalists, and family offices all represent key segments of this market. They are as diverse in their investment thesis and operational requirements as the assets they manage. Hedge funds may operate on high-frequency trading strategies while private equity firms engage in long-term value creation. Venture capital firms thrive on riskier, early-stage innovative bets while real estate and infrastructure players focus more on reliable physical asset and property management. As strategies and structures become more complex, to facilitate the business, there are further key players, service providers, and entities. This ecosystem of players and service providers in alternative investments is both complex and dynamic and each, with their actions and interactions, has important role to play in the lifecycle of the firms and the investments they manage. The following sub-sections identify these players and entities and outline the role they play.

2.2.1 Fund Administrators

Fund administrators provide several different services to a fund manager – fund accounting, that is, maintaining the financial books and records of the fund, investor statements and reporting, capital calls and distribution, fund NAV calculation, fund statements, tax-related works, etc.

They work closely with investor relations, deal-sourcing, portfolio-monitoring, and finance teams at different phases of the investment. Fund administration is a very critical and essential function for any alternative investment firm, and it requires closer integration with the firm's overall operations. There could be an inhouse team managing this function or could be outsourced to benefit from specialized expertise, technology, and cost efficiency in operations.

2.2.2   Co-investors

Co-investors can be existing LPs in a fund managed by the GP, or they can be new investors – in either case, these investors are looking for higher returns compared with fund returns. Co-investment is typically a non-controlling minority investment made by the investor directly in a company. As these investments are made outside of any fund structure, co-investors tend not to pay any management fees or carried interest on such an investment. From an alternative investment firm's perspective, co-investors are integral participants in the overall sphere of investment management, and their role should be reflected in the relevant accounting and management functions.

2.2.3   Accountants and Auditors

Accountants mainly prepare annual audited financial statements for the different funds managed by an alternative investment firm. Additionally, accounting firms can also help prepare management company financials, provide tax advice, assist in internal controls, and adhere to regulatory compliances. Such services add to fund expenses and hence unless mandated by regulations smaller alternative investment firms may opt for less frequent audits primarily to cut costs. With right systems in place, firms can reduce their dependency on accountants and auditors and achieve compliances within reasonable cost.

2.2.4 Agents and Advisors

Agents and advisors provide fundraising, fund placement, and advisory services to alternative investment firms – many of them have sizeable networks of relationships across diverse regions and sectors. Their roles enable fund managers to raise quality capital at a faster pace; allow private firms seek, time, and negotiate private capital; and they advise investors on placement of their private capital funds. Specific types of agents and advisors also offer advisory services on a portfolio company's management and divestment strategy and planning. Alternative investment firms need to have secure and reliable mechanisms to be able to share required information with their agents and advisors.

2.2.5 Consultants – Valuation and Compliance

A valuation consultant primarily assists in fair value reporting and ensuring that valuations meet accounting standards such as GAAP or IFRS. As part of their strategic advisory role, they may also develop and review valuation models applying appropriate methodologies such as discounted cash flow analysis, comparable analysis, and other industry-specific valuation techniques. Such a consultant may also help conducting due diligence on underlying assets and aid in firm's investment and divestment decisions. A compliance consultant has regulatory expertise and offers guidance on applicable regulations such as AIFMD, FATCA, etc. and plays a prominent role in regulatory filings and reporting. Their role is also to conduct compliance risk assessments, identifying areas of potential vulnerability and recommending corrective actions. Such a consultant may also assist in creating or enhancing the firm's compliance framework and implementing compliance testing and monitoring programs.

2.2.6 Legal Counsel

Legal counsels act as the guardians of the alternative investment firm's legal health. They have multiple responsibilities – regulatory compliance, due diligence for investment transactions, draft and negotiate contracts, assess, and mitigate legal risks, legal dispute resolution, protect intellectual property, employment, and workplace policies, etc. These functions cut across different teams and departments within a firm. Depending on the size of the firm alternative investment fund managers may utilize third-party law firms or have a small inhouse legal team.

2.2.7 Custodians

The primary role of a custodian is to hold the assets of a fund. The assets could be digital (stocks, bonds) or physical (real estate, art). Custodians are responsible for the settlement of trades and maintaining accurate records of all transactions and holdings. For some funds custodians may also provide additional services like NAV calculation, dividend processing, and corporate actions (e.g., rights issues, stock splits). The role of a custodian can vary significantly depending on the size of the alternative investment firm and the complexity of the assets under management. For a fund manager taking services of custodians, it is imperative to have an effective integration with their data and systems.

2.2.8 Special Purpose Vehicle

A special purpose vehicle (SPV) is deployed in alternative investments to contain a specific or temporary objective or function and is kept separate from the general partnership to isolate a potential financial risk. An SPV can take advantage of regulatory, legislative, and fiscal environment of the country in which it is set up, facilitating the private equity transactions in the geography of the investee company. There are various scenarios where participating funds can invest in target companies through one or more SPVs. They add an additional layer of complexity when it comes to private capital reporting, accounting, and tax-related matters. The concept of using protected cell company (PCC) as an SPV is also becoming prevalent in private capital domain.

2.2.9   Information Databases

These are the online agencies which provide the latest and comprehensive information needed at different points in the alternative investment cycle, saving professionals valuable time. They can source information on global investment firms, their funds return data, details of companies they have invested in and the associated investors and investment professionals. They can also provide latest news content or information, latest pricing and valuation information on potential deals and portfolio companies. Some alternative investment firms periodically review competitor deals, using data from databases – Capital IQ, FactSet, PitchBook, Prequin, Refinitive, and Bloomberg are a few examples – to have a better handle on future pipeline deals.

2.3   Global Market Structure – How Players Work Together?

Previous section has briefly touched upon how alternative investment segments (hedge funds, private equity firms, venture capitalists, fund of funds, and family offices) are diverse in their investment thesis, operational requirements, and the assets they manage. This diversity further increases with the region these firms operate in. Asia, Europe, North America, and emerging markets each present distinct characteristics, influenced by local regulations, accounting standards, compliance parameters, technological maturity, and investment culture. North America is a mature market with a robust technological infrastructure while Europe's market is characterized by a strong focus on regulatory compliance and leading in the adoption of environmental, social, and governance (ESG) factors. The Asia-Pacific region has technologically advanced nations like Japan and Singapore at one end, and emerging markets that are leapfrogging traditional investment models along with developing tech infrastructure at the other. With the previous section having defined the key players in alternative investments global market, it is now interesting to see the inter-relationships and how they work together. Figure 2.1 illustrates this association.

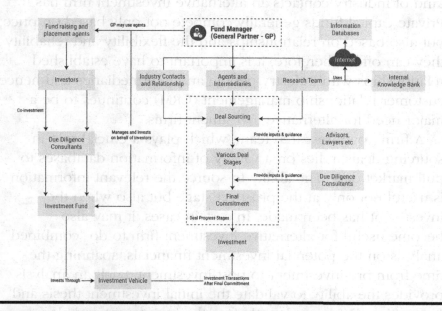

Figure 2.1   Inter-relationship and Association of Alternative Investments Market Players.

It is evident from Figure 2.1 that every single investment is a lengthy and complex process. Neither investors, the LPs, nor the fund manager, the GP (especially the small- and medium-size ones), are fully equipped to carry out all the activities on their own and need to rely on agents, consultants, service providers, and advisors before making some important decisions. Since they are not specialized in such tasks, they may not even want to invest their time but rather leave it to the experts. More the parties involved and hence more the need for legal compliance, information exchange, and security. Thus, engaging agents, advisors, and intermediaries give rise to several important complexities that fund managers have to be fully aware of. The fund manager should retain complete control over what information is provided to prospective investors (directly or via intermediate stakeholders) and the format in which such information is provided.

The general quality of deal flow is also dependent on the kind of industry contacts an alternative investment firm has. Private capital funds generally compete not only based on price, but also based on relationships and the flexibility and reliability they can offer. Therefore, it is important to have established relationships with industry people and intermediaries and hence customer relationship management (CRM) continues to be a major need for alternative investment firms.

A firm's own research team, which plays a crucial role in sourcing deals, relies on a variety of information databases to pull market data. The ability to source the relevant information is useful not only at the prospect stage but also when the investment has been made. In certain cases, it may also become useful for alternative investment firm to do "combined" analysis on the potential investment financials, spanning the time from pre-investment to post-investment. Such an analysis provides the ability to validate the initial investment thesis and forecasting that were done before the investment and also provides a continuum for the exit strategy from the investment.

Additionally, these information sources also enable effective analysis on how many deals have been closed in a region, the actual share a particular alternative investment fund managed to win, and why other deals were won by competitors.

Deal evaluation and due diligence is a multi-step and multi-player process and in alternative investments it has its own unique complexities. Advisors, lawyers, and consultants play indispensable roles in this process and this teamwork requires interdisciplinary collaboration and constant and secure flow of information back and forth.

The alternative investments market is a kind of mosaic where each player must fit in its right place. While investment strategies, asset types, operational regions are differentiators among alternative investment firms one thing that can be a great equalizer is "technology".

2.4 Structure of an Alternative Investments Management Firm – Who Does What?

So far various players in the alternative investment market have been discussed and their respective roles in the overall asset management lifecycle have been outlined. This section focuses on the functional structure within an alternative investment firm – the general partnership – that is, various departments and functions these departments are expected to perform. The structure of an alternative investments management firm is intricate, with each function critical to the overall functioning and success of the organization. Depending on the size of the firm a person and team may own more than one function while some functions may be outsourced. Irrespective of the size of the private capital firm, it is important to have a logical grouping of different functions under their respective heads. This section will elaborate the organizational structure of alternative investment firms.

Figure 2.2 shows all well-known, and some underlying, internal structural blocks between the different functional units/teams within an alternative investment firm. It is perfectly acceptable if there is some debate about whether certain functions are defined as core or support functions or whether they have a wider coverage than what is shown in Figure 2.2. It is also worth remembering that each alternative investment firm may have a slightly different team structure. The purpose of the figure is not-to-fit all alternative investment firms but to permit the audience to better understand impact of any changes on dependent and interlinked functional teams. Figure 2.2 does not attempt to represent any hierarchy but only the inter-relationship between the functional units.

The core and support units have been marked with their respective colors in Figure 2.2. Most support units work closely with multiple other units; however, there are some support units that may work specifically for a particular core business unit. Units such as information technology (IT), human resources (HR), and finance work and provide support to almost all the

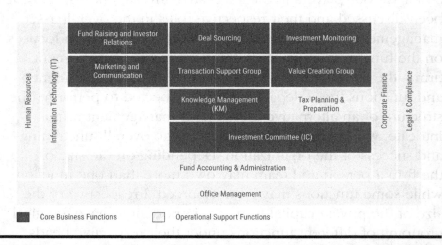

Figure 2.2 Association of Different Functional Units in an Alternative Investment Firm.

functional units. Each of the functional units and their points of interactions with other units are summarized in the following.

2.4.1   *Fundraising and Investor Relations*

This unit owns fundraising tasks like identifying potential investors, managing and communicating fundraising data and materials, and fundraising due diligence and investor relations management for existing investors. Management of investor communications including drawdown and distribution notices and handling investor queries is also owned by this unit.

2.4.2   *Marketing and Communications*

This group owns marketing of the firm's funds, branding, and external communication activities. It ensures that any messaging outside the firm is consistent and in line with the senior management of the firm. This unit would also typically own any information appearing on the external facing websites of the firm.

2.4.3   *Deal Sourcing*

The team managing deal sourcing or deal flow focuses on scouting, screening, and harvesting deals. The team members use their relationships, network of contacts and agents and advisors to find good investment opportunities at a good value. To access global information for comparison and analysis of sector and regional opportunities, they rely on online information databases and the knowledge management (KM) team. At later stages of a deal process, this team would interact with transaction support and funds team for correctly structuring the deal transactions.

2.4.4 Transaction Support Group

The transaction support group supports the deal team on all execution and structuring issues relating to transactions. Their expertise is helpful while setting up an SPV or SPVs as part of the deal structure. This group works closely with the deal team during the investment and divestment phases. In smaller funds, the transaction support team might not be a separate, specialized team. Instead, its functions could be integrated into investment team or finance team.

2.4.5 Knowledge Management

The KM or research team caters to the information needs of an alternative investment firm. This team manages, maintains, and makes available information about past deals, industry- and region-related news, competitor activities, industry trends, etc. They are one of the primary users of online information databases discussed in the previous section. In many smaller firms, the functions of KM might be part of the responsibilities of the investment team.

2.4.6 Investment Monitoring

Many alternative investment firms have dedicated teams that focus on monitoring and analyzing the performance of their investments. They maintain general information, comprehensive narrative commentary, and transaction details of investee companies for analysis and valuation purposes. The valuation process is also typically tied closely with investment monitoring. Accounting involves control of fund events and transactions occurring between funds and investee companies. Key attributes that are handled in accounting are purchases, disposals, gains/ losses, income accruals, and repayments.

2.4.7 Value-Creation Group

This is a group of operational experts who can work with investee company's management team to build value by driving operational and strategic improvements. The value-creation group supports the deal teams by identifying areas of potential improvement in prospective investments – for example, sales growth, margin improvement, and making and integrating acquisitions. Once the investment is made, the value-creation specialists work alongside management to achieve improvements, so that the value of each business is maximized. Smaller firms may rely more on external consultants or advisors, or value-creation tasks may become part of the broader responsibilities of the investment team.

2.4.8 Tax Planning and Preparation

Tax planning and structuring is crucial to any alternative investment firm since every transaction may have tax implications. The tax-preparation team, in large firms, is responsible for providing tax services such as preparation of tax returns, tax consulting for portfolio companies and the fund, and tax representation. From a tax-planning perspective they also own understanding principals' tax liabilities and goals, develop a plan to minimize tax liabilities, and enhance after-tax return on investment. They may also offer tax-planning advice to fund's investors. Smaller firms often outsource tax-related functions to external accounting or law firms specializing in tax matters or might be integrated into the broader responsibilities of the finance or legal team within the firm.

2.4.9 Investment Committee

The investment committee (IC) is the decision-making body for each fund of the alternative investment firm. Typically, investment and divestment proposals are prepared by the deal teams and approved by the IC after reviewing the proposals from various angles. Depending on the business process of a firm there could be more than one IC reviews for a deal before any decision is made. The IC may be consulted even during the life of investment in a portfolio on any material issue.

2.4.10   Fund Accounting and Administration

Fund accounting and administration team owns maintaining details of different fund structures, maintaining details (commitments, contacts, and bank details) of LPs and co-investors for each fund, track cash intake, maintain investor capital accounts, calculate distributions, preparation of investor communications, fund-level financial reporting, and similar fund- and investor-level accounting and administrative tasks. They work closely with investor relations, deal-sourcing, portfolio-monitoring, and finance teams at different phases of the investment.

2.4.11   Office Management

The office management team owns the maintenance of office facilities, working environment, and administration. This team is a major participant in business continuity planning (BCP) and testing program.

2.4.12   Finance

Finance is one of the critical and complex back-office functions in any alternative investment firm. They are responsible for corporate finance, firm-level planning and budgeting, operational expense, invoice management, consolidated financial reporting, fund recharges and expense management, financial audits, bookkeeping functions, account reconciliations, preparation of financial statements, and management of operating cash. They have touch points with almost every other unit within the firm and hence the obvious complexity.

2.4.13　Legal and Compliance

This team comprises legal advisors and lawyers and oversee the compliance/risk-management activities of the alternative investment firm. They support the firm's compliance with all relevant laws and rules and formulate required policies. They are also responsible for anti-money laundering (AML) checks and educating the employees in compliance/risk matters. The legal team becomes involved in due diligence at fundraising, deal screening, investment, and other phases as and when necessary.

2.4.14　Human Resources

Not so prominent in alternative investment firms (especially small- and mid-size houses) the HR team owns hiring, onboarding, employee data management, background checks, people policies formulation, feedback and appraisals, awards, remuneration, and other functions to take care of so valuable human capital.

2.4.15　Information Technology

Information, or IT, in any alternative investment firm typically has two distinct streams: infrastructure and information systems. Management of desktops, laptops, phones, mobiles, networking, cybersecurity, and servers is grouped under the infrastructure stream. Management of software, applications, and software products is grouped under information systems. BCP has IT as one of the critical areas to be included and addressed.

2.5 Increasing Role of ESG Criteria in Investment Decision-Making

There is a significant shift in how investors, companies, and regulators view the long-term sustainability and ethical impact of business activities, and it is clearly reflected in the increasing role of ESG criteria in investment decision-making of alternative investment firms. According to a recent LP survey conducted by INSEAD's Global Private Equity Initiative, 90% of LPs consider ESG factors when making investment decisions, and 77% of LPs use these factors when choosing GPs. This indicates that investors are looking for more information about the ESG impact of the assets in their portfolios and are actively seeking out companies with strong ESG practices.

According to the 2023 Global Private Equity Responsible Investment Survey, ESG has developed from a tool for risk management to a force behind wealth creation. Figure 2.3 depicts the main findings of this survey.

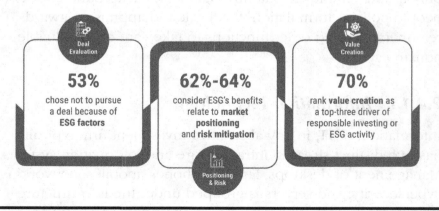

Figure 2.3 Global Private Equity Responsible Investment Survey, 2023.

As depicted in Figure 2.3, three main conclusions are as follows: Due to ESG considerations, 53% of respondents decided against pursuing a deal, 62%–64% believe that ESG benefits are related to risk reduction and market positioning, and 70% name "value creation" as one of the top three factors influencing ESG investing in private markets. This change in attitude demonstrates that private equity firms do recognize ESG as a transformational lever.

Alternative investment organizations require a trustworthy method for analyzing and rating different ESG criteria; yet ESG monitoring presents a number of difficulties, for example, lack of standardization in ESG parameters making it difficult to compare, many ESG factors are qualitative and challenging to measure and monitor consistently, ESG criteria and priorities can change rapidly. Technology is the only way to streamline ESG data and reporting for an alternative investment firm. While there are multiple technology solutions available in the market that support the collection of ESG data (both qualitative and quantitative) and analysis of raw data into actionable insights but not all solve the nuances of ESG data with respect to alternative investment market. Hence, it is imperative to evaluate those solutions that can combine financial and ESG monitoring and provide a more holistic view of an investment's health and prospects.

2.6 Summary

This chapter has described the different alternative investment market players, various functional units within an alternative investment firm, their high-level functions, interaction points, and dependencies on each other. They could broadly apply to a lot of private capital firms; while some may not have a very clear segregation, others may be managing fine without even having a couple of them. Chapters 1 and 2 have established a good context about the alternative investment industry global structure and private capital firm's internal operations. This information has been included to allow some readers who may be less familiar with the private capital market to find it useful to clarify some important and core terminologies. Due to a confluence of factors including investor demand, cultural changes, and legislative changes, ESG issues are becoming more and more important when making investment decisions. In subsequent chapters, the focus is going to be on identifying technical needs and a structured approach to address technical dilemmas that firms face before making an IT investment in their journey of technology transformation.

Bibliography

Comparison of the Costs and Features of the Four Leading Financial Data Providers: Bloomberg, Capital IQ (CapIQ), Factset and Refinitiv (www.wallstreetprep.com/knowledge/bloomberg-vs-capital-iq-vs-factset-vs-thomson-reuters-eikon/).

Global Private Equity Initiative (GPEI) by INSEAD (www.insead.edu/global-private-equity-initiative).

Global Private Equity Responsible Investment Survey 2023 (www.pwc.com/gx/en/services/sustainability/publications/private-equity-and-the-responsible-investment-survey.html).

Chapter 3

Technology Landscape in Alternative Investments

3.1   Introduction

Private capital firms have developed a track record as big investors in information technology (IT) firms, whether as investors in start-ups or relatively mature, cashflow-positive IT firms. Sequoia Capital and Accel Partners are among the most well-known global venture capital firms that focus on early-stage technology start-ups. Silver Lake is a good example of one of the leaders in private equity investment in technology and technology-enabled industries. Many of the leading companies in the IT industry have at one time in their history been funded by private equity and venture capital firms, underscoring the fact that private equity firms are aware of the strategic importance of technology as a driver of business growth. Since these investors have invested at different stages, they also

DOI: 10.1201/9781003481652-3

know the extent of transformation technology can bring to a business. Although private capital firms have continuously focused on their investor's interests and have constantly refined their investment strategy and plans, the irony is that they have not been very keen investors in information technology and technology infrastructure for their own firms. In their quest for success, many private capital firms have continued to rely on human intellect and effort with minimum support from technology. As private capital firms of different sizes will have varying technology needs, this chapter intends to explore and identify those different and sometimes overlapping areas.

3.2   Defining Systems and Technology Terminology

To define the subject matter more precisely, it is important to define and explain the key terms that will be used frequently in this chapter and throughout the publication.

3.2.1   Information Technology

IT is a general term that describes any technology that can produce, manipulate, communicate, and store information. Simply put, IT is anything that is concerned with technology to process information – hardware, software, networking, phones, and video conferencing. It is important to understand that IT in any organization typically has two distinct streams – infrastructure and information systems. The management of desktops, laptops, phones, mobiles, networking, and servers is grouped under the infrastructure stream while the management of software, applications and software products is grouped under information or business systems. Quite clearly only half of IT is about technology whereas the other half is about information. IT now includes many more aspects compared to its definition in past and hence it is important to understand this scope for both the IT streams especially for alternative investment firms where many people believe that IT is all about infrastructure side of things.

It is important to note that the term "system" used throughout this book refers to information systems and/or infrastructure systems.

3.2.2   *Architecture*

Almost everyone is familiar with the term architecture when it comes to a house or a building, and architecture in the context of a firm or organization is based on exactly the same concepts. Simply stated, architecture is anything that takes into consideration the needs and ensures those needs are met by the system design and properties. Architecture also ensures that it fits well within the operating environment it is part of and meets any regulatory rules. As with a building, various interrelated drawings (or models) are produced to depict how various needs will be met by the design (e.g., the floor plan, electrical plan, or air conditioning plan). Similarly, for an organization various architecture models are needed to depict how to meet the business needs, such as the business process view, data and information view, information systems view, security view, and technical architecture view. Defining the views from different stakeholders' perspective is what architecture is primarily about. Clearly architecture is not exclusively an IT term or task, rather creating architecture is more about thinking holistically and determining what makes sense for a particular firm. IT is an enabler for architecture components that require technology.

3.2.3   *Enterprise*

An organization (or cross-organizational entity) supporting a defined business scope and mission is an enterprise. An enterprise includes interdependent resources (people, organizations, and technology) that must coordinate their functions and share information in support of a common mission (or set of related missions). An enterprise could be a government agency, a whole organization, a division of an organization, a single department or a chain of geographically remote organizations linked by common ownership.

3.2.4 System Integration

Alternative investment firms may often use a variety of software systems for different functions such as deal management system, investment management system, CRM, and accounting system. System integration involves connecting these systems and making them talk to each other for streamlined operations. System integration can help achieve data consistency across systems, allows for more robust reporting and analytics capabilities, and can help the firm scale to accommodate growth. Some common methods used for system integration are API (Application Programming Interface) based integration, FTP (File Transfer Protocol) based integration, and ETL (Extract, Transform, Load) based data integration.

3.2.5 Business Architecture

A business has goals that it tries to achieve and in doing so executes a number of different functions and interactions with internal and external stakeholders of the business. In an alternative investment business, functions and interactions that investors see are different from what investees see, functions that the compliance team performs are different from what the finance team does and so on but eventually all such functions and units performing them should be structured and coordinated in a way that business is able to meet its overall goals and objectives effectively. This makes the business a complicated body. Business architecture (BA) aims to depict this structure, functions, and interaction in an easily understandable model that comprehends all the aspects of a business. Simplistically, BA typically involves defining what do we do; who does it; which information; where is it done; and what we want to achieve.

3.2.6 Customer Relationship Management

A customer or client relationship management (CRM) is a software program to help a business manage and organize its customer information. In the alternative investment context, a good CRM system will deliver capabilities encompassing deal management, investment management, fundraising and investor relations management. Not only is it a contacts directory (such as intermediaries, business partners, investors, and investee company management team) but it also has the ability to track customer interactions, manage internal and external communications, hence improving overall quality, efficiency, and profitability. Managing customer relationship is a business strategy for an organization and a CRM system is critical to implementing this strategy.

3.2.7 Document Management System

A document management system (DMS) is a computer system and software to store, manage, and track electronic documents and electronic images of paper-based information. Key features of a DMS are document upload/download, locking documents, security and access control, version control, rollback, audit trails, and intelligent search. An alternative investment firm will have document management needs to ensure a detailed history is stored for each limited partner (LP) including capital calls, distributions, capital account statements, financials, and others. Deal-flow and fundraising processes also have a lot of document management needs, such as linking the documents to individual deals, watermark documents before sharing with potential investors. Quick search and security are paramount features for any DMS in an alternative investment firm.

3.2.8   Enterprise Resource Planning

Enterprise resource planning (ERP) systems integrate internal and external management information across an entire organization. This information could span finance, accounting, sales, marketing, CRM, human resource management, supply chain management, and project management. ERP systems offer a lot of benefits in day-to-day operations, strategic planning, and others; however, they can be overly complex, extremely expensive, and difficult to integrate with other IT systems. Hence typically small-size alternative investment firms would manage without such a system, mid-size alternative investment firms would use only a sub-set of modules while large sized firms could implement a full-blown ERP system thus making the maximum benefit from the offering.

3.2.9   Data Warehouse

A data warehouse (DWH) system is a large store of data accumulated from a wide range of sources within an organization and used to guide management and operational strategies. DWHs are essentially databases that store current as well as historical data and are commonly used for creating trending reports for senior management reporting such as annual and quarterly comparisons. It allows analysis of data integrated from multiple, disparate operational systems. A well-designed DWH system may evolve into organization's "single source of truth" for a whole lot of data and information. At alternative investment firms, due to increasingly complex nature of investments and financial regulations, the amount of data stored and analyzed is rapidly increasing. A typical use of DWH in an alternative investment firm would be a detailed expenses report on funds by accumulating data from corporate financing system and fund accounting system which can be sliced and diced even for historical data. If an alternative investment firm has data in diverse sources, then ETL becomes a critical component of data warehousing strategy. ETL refers to the process of "Extracting" the data from different sources, "Transforming", that is, restructure it to make it suitable for analytical purposes, and then "Loading" the transformed data efficiently into DWH system.

3.2.10 Business Intelligence

Business intelligence (BI) is a set of applications and processes that transform raw data into meaningful and useful information used to enable more effective strategic, tactical, and operational insights and decision-making. Typically, BI applications use data from a DWH; however, not all DWHs are used for BI, nor do all BI applications require a DWH. In addition to having the capability of analyzing operational costs alternative investment firms can also use BI applications to draw real-time data from across their investee companies or funds and consolidate it to assess overall investment performance and also have a future-looking view. BI applications provide a consistent reporting and analysis approach, allowing investment analysts to effectively use their time in data analysis rather than pulling, collating, and generating graphs every time.

3.2.11 Software as a Service

Software as a Service (SaaS) is a software usage and distribution model in which applications are hosted by a vendor or service provider and made available to customers via web-based software over a network (the Internet). Customers do not own the software but obtain the license from the vendor to access and use it. These systems are typically priced on a per-user subscription basis along with the amount of data storage used. The SaaS model has several benefits, which include easier administration, global access, auto upgrades, and promised uptime. However, there are some adoption challenges for this model too – data security remains a concern since data is stored on vendor's servers, cannot be customized to meet specific business needs especially in the case of large alternative investment firms, and integration with other enterprise applications is complex.

3.2.12 Disaster Recovery/Business Continuity Plan

A Business Continuity Plan (BCP) is a roadmap for continuing operations of an organization under adverse conditions or disaster events. Such events could include a weather storm, building loss, major transport failure, loss of or damage to major computing or network resource. BCP involves analysis, design, implementation, testing, and maintenance of a disaster recovery (DR) solution. A business impact analysis (BIA) differentiates critical (urgent) and non-critical (non-urgent) organization functions/activities. Critical functions are those whose disruption is regarded as unacceptable. For each critical (in-scope) function, two values are then assigned:

- **Recovery Time Objective (RTO)** is the amount of time and a service level within which a business process must be restored after a disaster (or disruption) in order to avoid unacceptable impact to the business.
- **Recovery Point Objective (RPO)** is the point in time to which data must be recovered as defined by the organization. This is generally a definition of what an organization determines is an "acceptable loss" in a disaster situation.

Both RTOs and RPOs must be agreed with the respective business owners in the BCP. In the larger context, DR is focused on restoring the operations that are critical to keep the business running. From technology perspective, DR is commonly expressed as the minimum application and data requirements and the time in which the minimum application and application data must be available from the backups or failover data centers. This should also include phone systems, network connectivity, and mobile devices. Quite clearly BCP and DR are not only about technology, but technology does play a major role in the overall strategy.

3.2.13   Robotic Process Automation

Like any other industry, alternative investment firms also have a lot of repetitive and routine tasks such as payment processing, cashflow reconciliation, fee calculations, and data collection and processing. Usage of software robots (bots) to automate routine tasks not only frees up human resources for higher value activities but also minimizes errors and improves accuracy. Robotic process automation (RPA) has its own limitations also, for example, higher setup and implementation costs and its limitations to be effective for complex processes.

3.2.14   RegTech (Regulatory Technology)

Compliance is a major concern in the alternative investing space due to the continuously changing and complex regulatory landscape. "Regulatory technology" refers to how businesses can employ technology – especially advanced software and analytics – to comply with regulations effectively and affordably. In alternative investments, "RegTech" can be utilized for compliance monitoring and reporting, risk management, Anti-Money Laundering (AML), and Know Your Customer (KYC) processes, trade surveillance, data management, and security and regulatory change management. Integrating RegTech solutions with current systems is frequently necessary, but it can be difficult and resource intensive.

3.2.15 Natural Language Processing

A branch of artificial intelligence (AI) that focuses on enabling computers to understand, interpret, and respond to human language in a useful way. One of the key applications of natural language processing (NLP) in alternative investment space is analyzing financial reports, news, and social media for sentiment analysis. It can also be utilized in due diligence process, deal sourcing, investment management, automated reporting, and regulatory compliance. The quality of the data and the complexity of the algorithms utilized determine how well NLP applications perform.

3.3   Challenges for Alternative Investment Firms – How Do They Impact?

Before talking about the IT needs, let's look at a few challenges that influence the business operations of an alternative investment firm and may have impact on its core functions of fundraising and investments as well as other areas within the firm. These challenges are often a result of the complex nature of their investments, market dynamics, and operational issues.

3.3.1 Information and Knowledge Management

Finding good companies to invest in is not easy and it becomes even more difficult in developing countries where the information either does not exist or is obsolete. For some unlisted companies, financial information may not be fully regulated and there are no available checks for accuracy. As alternative investment firms grow, their information needs escalate as do the need for more researchers, industry- and function-specific experts, and access to journals and information databases. This lack of good-quality information at the right time does have several impacts including more time and effort in finding good prospects, more uninvested funds, inaccurate risk assessment, and longer due diligence cycle.

3.3.2 IT Systems Infrastructure

Many alternative investment firms have moved on from relying on excel sheets or inhouse systems for their core business functions (e.g., investment monitoring and fund-performance reporting) as well as support functions (e.g., corporate finance) and today they may have technologically advanced systems yet IT infrastructure remains a significant challenge for them. Alternative investment firms have constantly refined their investment strategy with a view to developing better techniques for management of deal flow or investment in the interest of their investors, but they haven't upgraded their IT strategy and infrastructure for their own firms with the same pace. Being a small-size firm or not being able to find a credible system (suiting specific needs) might be the reasons for not having upgraded systems, but not having a suitable IT systems infrastructure has several impacts such as report production is manual, time-consuming, and error-prone; fund-performance analysis is ad hoc; and an increase in the size of assets being managed warrants increase in the headcount at the general partnership. Having disparate systems leads to integration challenges, vast amount of data leads to data management challenges, newer technologies also bring newer security threats – so it's not just having the latest technology; it's about having an integrated, secure, and efficient infrastructure – and that still remains a challenge.

3.3.3 Regulatory Compliance and Reporting

Like every industry alternative asset has also been inching toward standardization of industry-specific guidelines with respect to ethical principles, compliance, and transparent reporting [e.g., the Global Investment Performance Standards (GIPS) and Institutional Limited Partners Association (ILPA) standards]. Monitoring compliance and ensuring consistency on an ongoing basis is a challenge for general partners (GPs) especially where data is to be accessed and collated from multiple sources. LPs are requiring more granular data to evaluate investment risks and meet compliance requirements at their end too. These divergent demands for information from LPs are increasing gradually and must be managed by GPs. If not managed timely and appropriately, the obvious impacts are an increase in the number of ad hoc requests from LPs to GPs; and it may work against the GPs in future fundraising.

3.3.4 Data Analysis

Alternative investment firms, irrespective of the size of assets they manage, have unique and advanced analysis and reporting needs. Whether looking at pipeline or investment or fund, it is critical for alternative investment firms to draw comparisons and analysis across various companies on desirable parameters to have meaningful real-time assessment of the performance. In parallel, it is equally important to be able to have a future-looking view of the investment performance by tweaking certain parameters that can change with time, for example, the investee company's or fund's financial data and currency fluctuations. Absence of such analytics makes defining the investment and exit strategies tougher for deal professionals and is more based on guess work rather than factual data.

3.3.5   Information on the Go

In the fast-moving world of financial services, there is no commodity more valuable than access to the right information at the right time. The uniqueness of the alternative investment model is that it is built around people who are only as effective as the communication channels they use and the information that they exchange on these channels. Effective and easy communications between deal makers, partners, portfolio companies, and other entities is the key at any alternative investment firm.

The team sizes in an alternative investment firm are small and at the same time each team needs information from other teams. The coupling between the teams is loose and a further challenge is that all the teams may be geographically distributed. Thus on-demand information is extremely relevant in an alternative investment context. The challenge is to be able to have access to both formal and informal information. Formal information may include pre-specified reports, contact information, or industry data. Information is needed when a deal team wants to look at relevant examples, historical data, the status of past deals, and learning on the fly. Informal information may include leveraging the industry or regional expertise of an individual while pursuing a deal that is not documented anywhere but is of immense value.[1]

3.3.6   Environmental, Social, and Governance (ESG) Factors

As discussed in the previous chapter, ESG factors have become increasingly important in the world of alternative investments. Their integration into financial performance analysis is complex and is a technical challenge while data availability and quality are operational challenges.

All alternative investment firms would have business goals to achieve and may be facing some or all the challenges listed earlier in their way to achieve those goals. One of the primary roles of an alternative investment firm's COO/CTO/ CIO is to make professional life easier for the firm's investment professionals. Therefore, business transformation (aided by technology) is needed to address these challenges and continue to find opportunities to increase efficiency at all levels and working to align technology with the firm's business objective. Not all the firms would have similar levels of inefficiencies and hence require a different tackling strategy, but it is imperative to first assess the current state of the business and then define the future state that the firm is striving to achieve.

The next section will delve into assessing a firm's technology requirements, guiding what to look from technology in making different business functions efficient and effective. During the technology selection process, firms and their stakeholders often encounter various challenges and uncertainties that can delay decision-making. The subsequent chapters will explore these dilemmas in depth, providing insights and guidance tailored to the unique context of each alternative investment firm, thereby aiding stakeholders in making well-informed decisions.

3.4   Technology Needs of Alternative Investment Firms

Each alternative investment firm should assess where technology can assist in delivering efficient operations and managing its funds throughout their lifecycle. This assessment should also consider the size and scale of the funds and investments being managed, and eventually become a necessary input to the technology strategy and vision needed for the organization. The requirements to manage increased volumes of quantitative and qualitative information grow in line with the numbers and size of the assets of the alternative investment firm. In the first quarter of 2022, Mergermarket conducted a survey among 30 senior executives, such as managing directors, data scientists, and Chief Technology Officers (CTOs), from U.S. Private Equity (PE) firms that manage assets of at least $2 billion. In the survey one of the questions was – *To what extent do you agree with the following statement: "Increased competition for assets is driving us to reassess our use of data and technology in our firm."?* Figure 3.1 shows the aggregated responses from those senior executives captured in the survey. As evident from Figure 3.1, PE firms want to stay ahead of the game since a significant portion of the survey participants (90%) concurred that increased competition for assets is compelling their firm to reevaluate its approach to data and technology usage. Among them, slightly more than a third (37%) expressed strong agreement with this assessment. Simply put, Excel spreadsheets or small inhouse systems can manage

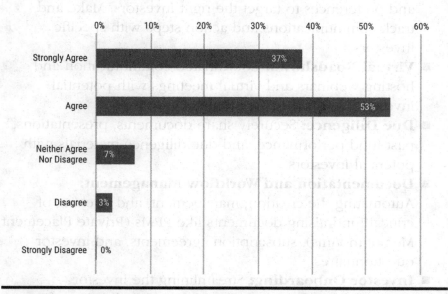

Figure 3.1   Increased Competition of Assets Is Driving Use of Data and Technology.

small funds and a limited number of investors, but as a fund grows it soon outgrows Excel's capabilities to effectively track and manage its complexities. Several areas are identified below where technology is needed and can bring tremendous value to the table.

3.4.1 Fundraising

Looking at the fundraising process and its several stages for alternative investment firms, there are multiple areas where technology is needed and can help. Listed here are some of such areas:

- **Marketing and Communication:** Contacts databases containing key and current information about investors to reach a broader audience and create awareness about the funds.
- **Investor Targeting:** Ability to analyze investor profiles and preferences to target the right investors. Make and track communications and action steps with specific investors.
- **Virtual Roadshows:** Coordinated communication and hosting webinars and virtual meetings with potential investors, using video conferencing tools.
- **Due Diligence:** Securely share documents, presentations, past fund performance, and due diligence materials with potential investors.
- **Documentation and Workflow Management:** Automating the creation, management, and tracking of critical fundraising documents like PPMs (Private Placement Memorandums), subscription agreements, and investor questionnaires.
- **Investor Onboarding:** Streamlining the investor onboarding process to facilitate smooth collection of

investor data, document signing, initial contributions and conducting KYC and AML checks.

■ **Capital Calls:** Make accurate and timely calls for capital and facilitate smooth and secure processing of investment transactions.

3.4.2 Deal-Flow Management

Deal-flow management is probably the most important function for any private capital firm. For every investment made, a private capital firm may process multiple deals – some rejected at the outset, some proceed to follow-up meetings internally and with owners, while some may stay active (i.e., remaining in progress) for many months. Deal opportunities with deals in progress have to be tracked across time zones and geographical regions. Multiple stakeholders are involved in the many aspects of a deal as it moves through various stages. Looking at the very nature of deal flow, it has some specific technical needs:

■ **Deal Sourcing:** Contacts databases containing key and current information about prospective investments/ investments and their key contacts. Scan the market and uncover new investment opportunities.

■ **Initial Screening and Risk Assessment:** Ability to track and categorize a deal's associated risk, investment size, probability, and business quality.

■ **Deal Evaluation and Analysis:** Search and compare potential deals against market benchmarks and past deals. Ability to do financial analysis and modeling to assess the viability and potential returns of a deal.

■ **Collaboration and Communication:** Cost- and time-efficient collaboration between deal teams, industry experts, investment committee, and lawyers throughout the deal process.

■ **Documentation and Workflow Management:**
Standardized and auto-generated documents and templates
that can be used to review deals. Manage the multiple
stages and tasks involved in progressing a deal through the
pipeline.
■ **Security:** For example, restricted access to work-in-
progress deals.

3.4.3 Investment Management and Fund Operations

Investment management and fund-operation process for an
alternative investment firm includes capture, administration,
use, and reporting of performance information of investee
companies (such as financials, ratios, and valuations). It also
includes control of fund events and transactions occurring
between fund(s) and investee companies. Alternative investment
firms typically receive a number of reports from their investee
companies on a monthly basis containing financials and other
performance data in different formats and structure. The firm
must then rekey data, calculate valuations and ratios, and create
summary reports. Alternative investment firm requires the
ability to work together with the management teams of investee
companies in creating value for their firms. The lack of reliable,
rich, and easy-to-use financial and business-performance
information of investee companies is particularly critical for
an alternative investment firm since it restrains its ability to
anticipate deviations and promote correcting actions, which
directly impacts the creation of value to their investors. Some
high-level technical needs can include the following:

■ **Investment Analysis and Monitoring:** Tracking and
managing a diverse range of investments across different
asset classes and geographies. Generate fund and
investment performance in an easy-to-understand and

review format. Handling various ratios for the allocation of the purchase and sale of investments.

- **Risk Management:** Access to key metrics of all investee companies, by fund and/or by industry for assessing various types of risk, including market, credit, liquidity, and operational risks.
- **Transaction Processing and Accounting:** Handling accurate plus cost and time efficient capital calls, distribution letters, quarterly reports, financial transactions, and fund transfers. Handling operating revenue and expenses, realized and unrealized profits and losses.
- **Investor Relations and Communication:** Enable investors and other permitted stakeholders to access fund information, report, and check the performance of investments.
- **Compliance and Transparent Reporting:** Highly granular reporting and analysis of the fund to cater to ever-increasing need to be more transparent to investors and adhere to compliance guidelines.
- **Asset Valuation:** Accurate and timely valuations and maintain a history of valuations from the valuation at date of initial investment to realization including a history of narrative commentary.
- **Exit Planning:** Investment and industry data analysis to assist in planning exit strategies.
- **ESG Integration:** Include ESG factors into investment analysis and reporting on ESG performance.

3.4.4 Support Operations

Support functions are huge enablers of the core business alternative asset functions. These include human resources, payroll management, corporate finance, staffing, office administration, and IT. They work together with core business teams or enable business teams, by providing data and systems to carry out business functions efficiently. The front-, middle-, and back-office activities would struggle to work efficiently in absence of strong and technology-enabled supporting functions. Some of the critical technical needs for support teams are among the following:

- **IT Infrastructure and Cybersecurity:** Provide fast, efficient, and reliable communication mechanisms to investment professionals. Security of information and implementation of adequate control and audit measures.
- **Accounting and Financial Management:** Corporate finance maintenance across the firm, track budgets, expenses, financial forecasting, and reporting. Prepare accurate tax returns and maintain tax basis of investments.
- **Human Resource Management:** Recruitments, onboarding, people appraisals, rewards, recognitions, payroll management, and trainings.
- **Operational Risk Management:** Identify, assess, and mitigate operational risks. Managing business continuity and DR plans. Undertake compliance education and compliance checks.
- **Administrative and Office Management:** Manage the procurement process, vendor selection, and contract management.

3.4.5 Knowledge Management

Knowledge is processed and meaningful inferences are derived from available data, which means information therefore is not always explicit. Explicit knowledge can be easily communicated and shared in the form of documents and data. However, this is only a very small percentage and knowledge of an alternative investment firm is deeply rooted in its people's insights, industry expertise, geographical experience, investor relations – this can be encapsulated as the firm's "intellectual capital". GPs with higher intellectual capital are able to attract better perception from LPs. Some of the technology needs in this area are among the following:

- **Search and Retrieval:** Immediate, reliable, and quick delivery of information to investment managers in a self-serve manner.
- **Data Collection and Aggregation:** Integrated view of data from across and even outside the organization.
- **Decision Support Systems:** Future vision from historical trends and analytics, for example, deals lost to competition and time spent on deals.
- **Information Processing and Analysis:** Tools for looking at data in new ways, that is, slice-and-dice analysis and a forward-looking view of investment performance.
- **Multi-channel Information:** Information on the go, for example, updated investor contacts information and key industry experts' details.

By no means are the technology needs identified in the previous sections exhaustive. These are some potential areas where IT can be a real enabler and add tremendous value to the whole business function. Obviously, the exact needs would differ from one alternative investment firm to another, but these high-level areas would typically be applicable to a large section of alternative investment firms.

For smaller and mid-sized alternative investment firms, technology can automate most of the front- and back-office operations. For large firms, due to diversity in the types of funds, different sectors, regions, investor clauses, and calculation models, achieving full automation could be a challenge. Hence in such scenarios it helps to apply Pareto's Principle (the famous 80-20 rule) to identify the extent of automation that will provide maximum benefits and not trying to fit in every requirement in a system.

3.5   Technology Dilemmas of Alternative Investment Firms

Technology across the globe is moving ahead at a very rapid pace – in terms of both number of options and capabilities of those options. In the last decade, even in alternative investment space, there are plethora of technology options and hence the firms face several dilemmas:

- What to automate? How to decide which processes within alternative investment firms should be automated.
- What services/solutions to choose? Build versus buy and the extent of customization.
- Where to run the systems? On-premises versus cloud-based solutions.
- Cost versus Value – Is automation worth the cost? The Return on Investment (ROI) uncertainty.
- How to access the information and systems? Fine balance between ease of access and security.
- How to approach technology transformation? Big bang or gradual rollout and adoption.

Technology is both a strategic asset and a challenge; hence, addressing these dilemmas requires a strategic approach, often involving a hybrid solution that optimizes across various dimensions to meet the unique needs of the firm. Next few chapters will delve into the pros and cons of each aspect of the dilemmas faced by firms and attempt to help alternative investment firms take the right decision for them.

3.6   Summary

Alternative investment firms need to manage increased volumes of quantitative and qualitative information that grow in line with the number and size of their funds and investments. Looking at the different areas highlighted in this chapter, technology can surely enhance the efficient operation and management of funds; however, it is important that alternative investment firms make assessment of where technology may rightly assist them. The assessments drive the decisions like buy or build and evaluate what would fit best for the specific needs. Having now looked at alternative investment firms' technology needs and dilemmas, the next few chapters will focus on bringing out different perspectives that can help do this assessment.

Note

1 There are many other factors that may influence the investments and on-the-ground operations of an alternative investment firm including political, legal, socio-cultural, geographical, and talent retention which require an organizational strategy to tackle such challenges. Hence due to the very nature of such challenges these are not being discussed in this book.

Bibliography

Private Equity's race for data (www.spglobal.com/marketintelligence/en/mi/info/0522/private-equity-race-for-data.html)

Chapter 4

Technology Dilemma 1: What to Automate?

4.1 Introduction

Though it wasn't the case always but for last one decade technology is advancing at a great pace in the world of alternative investment, presenting both enormous opportunities and challenges. Technology in alternative investment space has evolved from being an afterthought to an integral part of the sector and especially post-COVID-19 automation is becoming a pivotal factor in alternative investment firms to enhance efficiency, reduce costs, and improve accuracy.

It's always a topic of discussion whether the investments made by alternative investment firms, based on their thesis and strategies, are elements of science or art. The discussion could go either way; however, a firm's philosophy could largely depend on the investment type, for example, quantitative hedge funds tend to rely more on statistical models and data-driven frameworks, focusing on scientific approaches, while

 DOI: 10.1201/9781003481652-4

private capital firms, such as venture capital and private equity, are more likely to depend on the experience, intuition, and qualitative judgments of their investment professionals. And hence when it comes to deploying technology, alternative investment firms are faced with a basic dilemma of maintaining the balance between innovation and tradition, that is, determining which processes within alternative investment firms should be automated to balance efficiency with the human touch. What parts of their operations should they automate, and where can they use technology to its greatest potential?

4.2 Human Capital or Business Knowledge Codification – What to Rely Upon?

Section 3.3 in Chapter 3 highlighted a few challenges that influence the business operations of an alternative investment firm:

- Information and Knowledge Management
- IT Systems Infrastructure
- Regulatory Compliance and Reporting
- Data Analysis
- Information on the Go
- Environmental, Social, and Governance (ESG) Factors

These challenges span all the critical functions, including fundraising, deal management, investment monitoring, and accounting, and information from one feed into another. Over a period, different teams within the firm may have adopted different applications to support their own key processes and functions while some might still be relying on Excel spreadsheets and other manual administration of tasks. They might have their own checks and balances but eventually there would be multiple sources of structured and unstructured data with none being the single source of truth. They might be able to generate Limited Partner (LP) reports gathering information from multiple resources but unable to reference the data used to generate them. They might be able to perform their daily functions but with consistent overreliance on individuals across the teams. These collective skills, knowledge, experience, and expertise that employees bring to an organization is referred to as "human capital" and it is the backbone of the alternative investment industry.

Human capital drives decision-making and also plays a crucial role in building and maintaining investor relationships. But depending only on human capital has its own set of challenges. Important worries include the possibility of knowledge loss because of staff turnover, inconsistent decision-making, and the limitations in scaling expertise. Alternative investment firms must look at "business knowledge codification" to address these challenges. Codification is the process of converting tacit knowledge into information that is easy to reproduce, reduces uncertainties and asymmetries, and more importantly is independent of people. Business knowledge codification is a systematic approach to documenting, organizing systematizing business knowledge for efficient sharing and utilization.

It's important looking at how alternative investment stacks up against other finance domains when it comes to "codification" using technology. The codification process may entail high initial efforts and fixed costs, to bring knowledge onto documents, to set up stable systems, but then gradually allows people to carry out operations at very low costs. Figure 4.1 depicts a relative comparison of alternative investments domain with other finance domains with respect to business intelligence codification using technology. All domains are leveraging technology but the extent to which different domains can achieve codification through technology leverage is worth looking at. Big IT service providers have dedicated

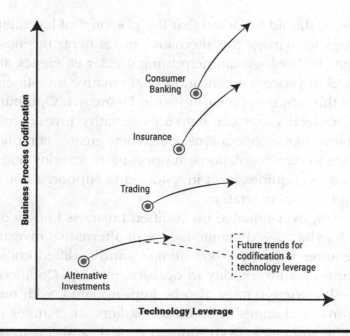

Figure 4.1 Business Process Codification and Technology Leverage Quadrant.

business verticals to support their banking and insurance clients but there is hardly any large enough IT service provider that would have an alternative investment vertical. It shows that codification in alternative investments still has a long way to go.

Quite clearly, although the use of technology is increasing in alternative investments, it is still lagging in terms of both codification and technology usage. Many would agree that the business process codification in an alternative investment scenario cannot be achieved beyond a certain point, which is in part due to the ad hoc nature of processes and in part due to the uniqueness of each deal. In contrast to this, investment banking or consumer banking are domains where a higher level of codification can be achieved because business rules are largely predefined and can be embedded in the systems.

However, it should be noted that the potential of leveraging technology to manage the alternative investments business is very high. Technology can help bring greater efficiency at the same level of process codification in alternative investments, which is the future trend as shown in Figure 4.1. Optimum leverage of technology can help an alternative investment firm achieve higher operational efficiency, greater compliance, adherence to new regulations, support more scrutiny and handle more enquiries from investors, and support a constantly evolving investment strategy.

However, over-reliance on codified business knowledge has its drawbacks – dynamic nature of alternative investments often requires out-of-the-box thinking and codified knowledge can at times lead to rigidity in decision-making. Codified business knowledge must also be kept updated, with new regulations or changes in financial markets, or changes in investment strategies. Both "human capital" and "business knowledge codification" play a pivotal role in taking the business ahead in alternative investment firms. On one hand, the value of human capital in alternative investments cannot be undermined where strategies and decisions often require a high degree of personal insight and discretion, and at the same time scalability, consistency, and data-processing abilities of automated systems are essential to the growth of any firm. While codified knowledge provides consistency and is more adept at handling quantitative data without fatigue or bias, human capital excels in qualitative analysis and relationship management. Considering the unique aspects of alternative investments, one cannot be chosen over another; hence a blend of both is usually the most effective strategy. It is a dynamic balance and in this industry of continuous learning, and if human intellect is regularly fed into the systems (i.e., codified), then demand of constant innovation can be met in a process-oriented way.

4.3 Why Move from Static to Systematic Information Management?

Effective information management is essential for success in the rapidly evolving world of alternative investments. Traditionally, alternative investments have relied on static methods of information management – spreadsheets, isolated data silos, and standalone systems. Static systems may be manual or semi-automated and they lack the dynamism needed to handle the vast and varied data in the alternative investment space. Such systems carry the risk of errors, outdated information, and slow response times. However, in last 10–15 years things have changed and apps like customer relationship managements (CRMs) are now considered table stakes but if they are not integrated with other systems, then they fall in the category of standalone systems.

A survey was conducted by S&P Global Market Intelligence in 2021-2022 across Private Equity (PE) and Venture Capital (VC) practitioners globally to measure industry outlooks for the upcoming 12 months. In this survey they also included a question on PE and VC firms' advances on their digitization and automation journey – "Looking at digital transformation and automation efforts across workflows, in your opinion, where does your organization currently stand in this journey?" Responses from the survey are shown in Figure 4.2 and it clearly shows that regions across the world are at different stages of digital technology adoption. Overall, 41% of respondents state that their companies are still in the early phases of implementation, mostly concentrating on the use of digital platforms for reporting and CRM. About advanced digitization, 14% of respondents stated their companies have progressed to the point where they are using data science for automated due diligence and deal sourcing, while only 7% said digital technologies are fully integrated into their playbook.

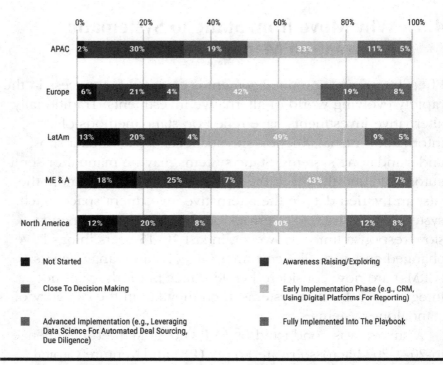

Figure 4.2 Digital Transformation and Automation across Workflows Globally.

Across the regions, the industry is branching out and experimenting with more advanced applications concerned with data analytics and investment team workflows. Systematic information management can adapt to new information, process large datasets, integrate new data streams, and provide real-time insights that leads to better-informed decision-making and can be a competitive advantage in the rapidly evolving market.

Since systematic information management is defined by automated, integrated, and dynamic processes some of the tangible benefits that it can bring are operational efficiency, reduced costs and time for diverse tasks, and quality information. However, that is not all as it can generate considerable intangible value that may not be directly correlated to dollar values. Real-time pipeline and portfolio graphical analysis, slicing and dicing data, security, and fluid digital communication with investors are just some examples.

Transitioning from static to systematic information management may face resistance from users, which if not addressed upfront can lead to the failure of the overall transformation program. Although each alternative investment firm will have its own unique hurdles, Table 4.1 highlights those typical to each firm.

It is clear from Table 4.1 that collaboration and respective team contribution are the key challenges, which if conquered ensure people are aligned to the transformation program.

Additionally, effective training can really help team members to adapt to new systems. Depending on the existing infrastructure, integrating systems together could be complex, time taking, and resource intensive but with team members onboarded that's an investment that definitely pays off in the long term.

4.4 Automation – Always Gets Better with Time

"Automation", defined as digital transformation of the business process, can be intimidating to many as it seems like a binary switch – either entirely on or off. So, it's important to first clearly define the term "automation" or "digital transformation" from an organization's perspective. Transformation is all about moving the performance dial, at the right time, using the right tools to deliver the best results. Business transformation's key objective is to achieve a step-change in an organization's capabilities. Practically, transformation is not necessarily about starting from scratch and redoing everything but is rather about focusing on the bigger picture and being able to achieve sustainable business transformation by:

Table 4.1 Common Challenges/Conflicts Encountered During System Implementation Projects

Challenges/Conflicts	Resolving Method/Argument
Business is happy with the current spread sheets for fund accounting so what's the need to change. **Challenge:** Resistance to change.	Spread sheets no longer cut for strategic direction we want to move in. We can't afford to lose our precious time in revalidating and formatting data all the time, which is a growing pain.
Our investment model is too complex to document, and we anyway know it in and out. **Challenge:** Documenting the business knowledge.	There are great advantages of the experience you have but you assume everyone has the same level of knowledge as you do. As our organization grows and our staff expands, there is a greater need to maintain the same level of knowledge. We can start with documenting and it surely be improved with time. It will result in precious information assets that can be leveraged later in multiple ways.
We deal with corporate finance and for anything to do with fund-level accounting please talk to relevant team. **Challenge:** Making functional units collaborate with each other without political resistance.	In such scenarios nurturing C-level acceptance and go-ahead definitely helps. Additionally defining different work streams and assigning champions to each (from different functional units) also helps.
Not enough or minimal documentation about existing processes, functions, business rules, etc. **Challenge:** No existing documentation; how to document gaps?	If AS-IS documentation doesn't exist, then focus on TO-BE and ensure it is documented well.

Source: Author.

- leveraging what already exists;
- adopting the 80/20 rule;
- acting fast; and
- showing incremental transitions with measurable benefits.

Contrary to popular belief, automation is a continuous process that constantly evolves and gets better with time and even in alternative investments firms it is not a one-time, static exercise. Machine learning and artificial intelligence are great examples of how systems can learn and improve from each cycle of data they process. They can only get better, more efficient, and more accurate with time. Within alternative investment industry algorithmic trading, predictive analytics for investment opportunities, and automated regulatory compliance checks are great examples of how automated systems have evolved with time.

Like in any other industry no one can claim in alternative investments that business model and investment strategy is going to remain constant for the next three to five years. Likewise, no one can claim that the environment – encompassing investors, competitors, regulations, and tax laws – is not going to change in the near-to-long term. Hence it is imperative to have a continuous process of translating business vision and strategy into processes and models that are effective, efficient, agile, durable yet adaptable to future changes. Alternative investment firms should start with basic automation and as they become comfortable progressively build on the previous step of automation to move to the next one, that is, firms should build on the concept of iterative improvement.

Starting point for automation depends on where a company currently stands in terms of digital maturity. Hence some suggested key considerations for identifying the starting point would be:

- **Assess Processes:** Analyze existing processes and ask questions like:
  o What are the biggest bottlenecks in our processes?
  o Where are redundancies and inefficiencies in our processes?
- **Identify Needs:** Based on these questions identify the most pressing business needs that automation can solve such as data accuracy, document management, reporting, or communication.
- **Refine Processes:** Refine the process (if required) and document in a clear, concise, and easy-to-follow manner.
- **Evaluate As-is Tech:** Evaluate current technological infrastructure to leverage what already exists.
- **Create Plan:** Create a project that can be a quick win. Quick wins can build momentum and support for further automation efforts.
- **Plan Training:** Also plan for training and change management since employee buy-in is crucial for the successful adoption of new technologies.
- **Choose System:** Choose the new technology system keeping in consideration that this early automation choice:
  o Does not limit future expansion or integration.
  o Complies with relevant financial regulations and standards.
  o Offers necessary data security and privacy features.
- **Kick Off the Project:** Set clear, achievable goals for the initial phase of automation and kick off the project.

Having looked at some considerations for identifying the starting point it's time to look at few possible scenarios in context of private capital firms:

- **Scenario 1:** A private debt firm having complex amortization schedules, which are becoming increasingly difficult to manage, might consider prioritizing the automation of their most used amortization schedule model within the firm. Learnings from the initial automation can then be leveraged to automate all the models and achieve 100% automation in this specific function of the firm. When choosing the system for amortization schedule automation they must probably keep future integration with fund accounting in consideration.

■ **Scenario 2:** A private equity firm may begin with Microsoft Excel and a generic accounting package for its back-office needs for first one or two funds. As the number of funds grow and fund structure become complex inefficiency starts creeping in. Firm would need to find a solution to be able to scale and support the rapid growth of the firm. A logical initial step would be to choose a fund accounting system that either has additional modules inbuilt for future use or supports integration and facilitates the seamless exchange of data both into and out of the system.

■ **Scenario 3:** A venture capital firm having a few investors could manage LP reporting with Microsoft Office and a shared drive. However, as the firm's client base expands and grows to hundreds of investors the traditional methods won't be able to keep up. More sophisticated LPs are also going to require more sophisticated reporting; hence MS Office based reporting and communication will not take them far. VC firm could initiate exploring Investor Portal solutions that will not only bring efficiency in their process as well as elevate the experience of its investors. Investor Portal solution should have its own CRM or integrate well with firm's existing CRM to take the automation to the next level in subsequent phases.

■ **Scenario 4:** A fund of funds in the initial stages might be primarily relying on manual processes for data analysis and reporting of their investee funds and their underlying investments. As the number of investee funds grow data collection and analysis would consume considerable time and are prone to human error. The firm could aim to improve the efficiency and accuracy of its data-related processes by implementing a basic data management and analytics tool and automating data collection and basic analysis tasks. The selected tool should be capable of integrating with advanced AI and ML technologies down the line, as well as with other systems, to consolidate data for thorough and comprehensive reporting.

Rajdeep Endow, Chief Transformation Officer and Private Equity Advisor, puts it nicely when he says:

> Automation in alternative investments as well as any other domain is a journey. It takes time to integrate and fine-tune new technologies and systems, but with each step forward, we see improvements in how we manage processes. As we continue to refine these processes, automation becomes more effective and indispensable. It's a process that builds on itself – getting better, smarter, and more efficient as time goes on.

4.5 Summary

Traditionally, the private capital markets have been characterized by manual operations and workflows. The direction of investments is often steered by investment professionals who bring years of experience and a deep understanding of the markets. This chapter has emphasized on the importance of finding the right balance between leveraging human capital and embracing technology. Approach to automation should be strategic, one that complements human expertise rather than trying to replace it. While the decision to automate and transform is complex but if done with a well-devised plan and the backing of stakeholders then benefits of automation in alternative investments can be substantial. Automation is a journey and once started it's important to continuously monitor, solicit feedback, and refine processes to ensure that they remain effective.

Bibliography

Global Private Equity Outlook Survey (2022) (www.spglobal.com/mar ketintelligence/en/news-insights/research/2022-global-private-equity-outlook)

Chapter 5

Technology Dilemma 2: What Services/Solutions to Choose?

5.1 Introduction

In the dynamic landscape of alternative investments, technology plays a pivotal role in shaping operational efficiencies and investment outcomes. Previous chapters so far have discussed the operational challenges faced by alternative investment firms and technology needs of the firms to address the challenges. Chapter 4 covered identifying bottlenecks in the business processes, prioritize the functions for automation, set clear objectives with outcomes and define the project(s) for automation. A crucial decision that firms face at this point is selecting the right technology services and solutions that align with their unique business processes and goals. There may be a plethora of choices available, each promising enhanced

 DOI: 10.1201/9781003481652-5

efficiency, security, and competitive edge, but the selection process requires a strategic foresight and a balance between cost, capability, security, and future scalability. This chapter and the next few chapters will contextualize these technology dilemmas and help the alternative investment professionals take the right calls in this critical decision for their firms.

5.2 One Integrated Solution or Multiple Small Systems?

As discussed in Chapter 3, IT in any organization typically has two distinct streams: infrastructure and information systems. The management of desktops, laptops, phones, mobiles, networking, and servers is grouped under the infrastructure stream while the management of software, applications, and software products is grouped under information or business systems. In small- and mid-sized alternative investment firms, IT infrastructure requirements are very basic, for example, a reliable network setup, basic cybersecurity measures, few printers, conferencing setup, laptops for team members with essential tools like standard office software, email access, and cloud-based storage solutions – Dropbox, OneDrive, or Google Drive. Larger firms would also have a few on-premises servers, localized shared drive, advanced security setup with firewalls, and multiple networks. It would not be an overstatement to say that these components form the backbone of the organization, and these are selected, set up, operated, and managed by inhouse or outsourced IT team. These are essential for an alternative investment firm to operate but when it comes to operational efficiency of investment professionals, information systems become pivotal. Hence the focus of this section would be on information systems in alternative investments domain.

Anyone who would have explored alternative investment technology solutions would have probably heard the terms "end-to-end", "integrated", "comprehensive", "enterprise level", "best-of-breed", "modular", etc. to describe the solutions available in the market. It's important to be very clear about not only their common meaning in the alternative investment marketplace but also the context in which a solution provider has used these terms in its pitch. Simply put an integrated or end-to-end or comprehensive software would mean that most of the business data is captured, processed, and analyzed within one technology solution. They may also be referred to as "enterprise level" systems that can serve front, middle, and back office. On the other hand, specialized software tailored for specific functions represent the "best-of-breed" systems since they offer depth in their respective functions.

The decision around adopting a single integrated solution versus multiple specialized systems is a strategic one and hence needs a detailed discussion. Table 5.1 lists down various decision factors that should be considered in this strategic decision. Business user adoption is critical to the success of any technical system implementation. An integrated or end-to-end solution can offer a uniform and seamless user experience, which simplifies training and leads to a better adoption within business teams. Multiple systems will have their own varied interfaces and hence training would vary and probably take longer too.

Budget and cost often become the decisive factors in the selection process of technology systems. Cost could have multiple components – licensing, implementation, customization, migration, training, and support. If the deployment model is on-premises, then hardware or hosting cost is also a component. An integrated system may require substantial investment initially (especially in on-premises deployment); however, over time, the investment in integrated,

Table 5.1 Integrated System versus Best-of-Breed Systems

Decision Factors	Integrated System	Best-of-Breed Systems
User Experience and Training	Uniform user experience, simplified and one time training	Varied and multiple times training
Initial Cost	More	Less (for each system)
Long-Term Cost	Less	More (for all systems)
Data Integrity and Interoperability	Single source of truth, one-integration solution	Requires data integration and reconciliation
Scalability and Flexibility	Easily scalable, fairly flexible	Requires robust integration, more flexible
Data Security and Permissions	Centralized control	Distributed within each system
System Failure Risk	Potential for Widespread System Failure	Reduced Risk of Total System Failure
Overall Architecture/ Tech Stack	Consistent and cohesive	Can become disjointed and complex
Support	One support/vendor team	Multiple support/ vendor teams

Source: Author.

multi-purpose technology will reduce the need for multiple vendors and will gain the efficiencies through streamlined processes which can offset the upfront cost. SaaS (or pay as you go) model largely takes care of this upfront cost concern. Conversely, multiple best-of-breed systems might appear cost-effective at the outset since systems are implemented incrementally; hence the cost spreads out over a longer period.

But eventually the cost of multiple systems adds up in the long run. The cost can further escalate due to the need for custom integrations and data reconciliation.

Data accuracy and integrity are paramount in alternative investment firms for several reasons – it's crucial for assessing investment opportunities, conducting due diligence, risk assessment, fulfilling regulatory compliance, gaining investor confidence, and maintaining its reputation in the ecosystem. An integrated solution offers a single source of truth across the firm. Firms can hugely benefit from accurate and unified reporting through this unified and singular data repository thus enhancing decision-making and regulatory compliance. Multiple specialized systems approach can lead to data silos and integration challenges. With multiple systems, ensuring data integrity requires robust integration and reconciliation processes and alternative investment firms may face increased costs and time spent on system interoperability and data reconciliation. Thus, with best-of-breed systems strategy, firms must be prepared to invest time and money in ongoing integration work to prevent operational fragmentation.

Alternative investments are a competitive and ever-changing market. Firms grow; and in the dynamic landscape of alternative investments their investment strategies change and thus IT needs also evolve. Hence when an alternative investment firm evaluates its technology options, it should adopt a forward-looking perspective. The technology chosen today must not only meet present needs but also allow for expansion and changes in the market in the future. Alternative investment firms need to be agile, prepared to review and adjust their IT strategy in response to new developments and changes in their corporate goals. Integrated or end-to-end systems are capable of effectively scaling up to accommodate higher user and data volumes without requiring substantial structural modifications. However, when it comes to incorporating new and cutting-edge technologies or adjusting to shifting market conditions or new regulatory requirements, they might be less adaptable. On the other hand, firms might theoretically stay at the forefront of business changes and innovation by plugging in new technology as needed thanks to the patchwork approach of several small systems. However, making sure the various systems can interact robustly and efficiently without creating data silos or operational bottlenecks is the difficult part, though. When it comes to scalability and flexibility, firm's long-term vision is also critical. An alternative investment firm focused on rapid and robust growth may prefer the scalability of an integrated solution, while a firm aiming for flexibility and rapid adoption of best-in-class technologies might opt for multiple specialized systems.

Given the sensitive nature of their operations, for an alternative investment firm, criticality of compliance with financial regulations and the need for robust data security is vital. They may start with basic technology setup but with the increase in team size or need to handle larger volumes of data security demands increase. An integrated system offers a centralized control and management of user roles and permissions on data which also allows for easier periodic reviews and changes. In the case of multiple systems, the burden of maintaining security rules consistently across a diverse set of systems can be significant. However, when it comes to availability and uptime, having multiple systems reduces the risk of total system failure, as issues in one system don't directly impair others. An integrated system brings a significant dependency on a single system, which can be a critical point of failure, but if infrastructure redundancy and disaster recovery is planned well, it's not a differentiating issue.

Integrated technology solutions typically necessitate agreement from multiple teams on the final purchasing decision because they are intended for usage by several teams. To bring all the stakeholders on the same page could be tedious and lengthy. On the other hand, best-of-breed solutions are usually designed for a single purpose, which makes getting majority buy-in easier. However, when teams start buying technology independently of each other the overall technological stack may get complex, jumbled, and unmanageable. Such a disjointed IT stack results in lost money, time, and resources.

Business users need support when using a system – it could be around data upload, queries from new users, or any system malfunction. Customer support can become messy when a firm uses several different technologies or systems as users may have to reach out to each of the unique support teams. If an issue requires more than one solution team to work on, then business user would even have to serve as the point of contact for different vendors. However, with an integrated solution, the support team is single and is well versed in the entire range of capabilities within the application.

So how can an alternative investment firm take the right call? The decision between an integrated solution or multiple specialized systems is not merely a technological choice but a strategic one that will shape an alternative investment firm's operational capabilities and strategic agility. With a comprehensive understanding of these considerations, alternative investment firms can approach the decision-making process with a balanced view and carefully weigh the immediate and long-term benefits and challenges of each approach. A firm must evaluate its priorities – whether it is cost savings, operational efficiency, data integrity, user experience, or flexibility – and determine which technology strategy best supports these objectives. Ultimately, the choice must align with the firm's operational goals.

5.3 Technology Systems/Services Available in Alternative Investments Market – Do They Solve Everything?

Technological solutions and services have shown a significant increase in the alternative investment industry, which are designed to enhance decision-making, quicken operations, and ensure compliance. These range from customer relationship management (CRM) software to complex portfolio management systems. This section gives an outline of the technology systems and services that are currently used in the alternative investment market. Yet it is only a limited set. Even when some of the systems mentioned might be the market leaders, the lists provided here do not rate, rank, or compare the different systems in any way.

In fact, one can say that the alternative investments information systems market is concentrated around a few suppliers employing broad, multifunction strategies, and a larger group that provides specialized products. This distribution can be named a "barbell" distribution with a lot of specialist service suppliers on one side and a small number of integrated multi-function product companies on the other.

As seen in Tables 5.2, 5.3, and 5.4, the current market offers a variety of solutions tailored to the alternative investment sector and they have specific focus areas – front, middle, or back office. For instance, there are platforms specifically designed for fund accounting, investor reporting, risk management, and deal-flow tracking. Systems like these are rich in features that cater to the unique requirements of private capital firms. On the other side, Table 5.5 lists some systems that offer integrated or end-to-end functionalities.

It is important to understand that while these systems, best-of-breeds and integrated, offer a lot of functionalities, they have their downsides. One example is that a CRM system may be

Table 5.2 Software Solutions Providers (Front Office)

System/Provider Name	High Level Solutions[a]
4Degrees	CRM, Relationship Intelligence, Deal Flow
Affinity	CRM, Deal Flow, Relationship Intelligence, Investor Relations
Datasite	LP Portal, Reporting
DealCloud	CRM, Deal Pipeline, Fundraising, and Investor Relations
Monday.com	CRM, Sales Pipeline, Project, and Task Management
Salesforce	CRM, Deal Pipeline

Source: Compiled from various provider websites and tool comparisons.

[a] This list comprises a selection of high-level solutions relevant to the scope of this publication, based on information available from the solution providers' websites and other online resources as of the time of writing. Please note that some specific features or solutions may not be included due to the breadth of offerings in the industry and the dynamic nature of technology.

Table 5.3 Software Solutions Providers (Middle Office)

System/Provider Name	High Level Solutions[a]
Acquity Knowledge Partners	Portfolio Management, Fund Operations
Burgiss (now MSCI)	Portfolio Monitoring, Company Benchmarks, Performance Benchmarks
Cobalt	Portfolio Monitoring, Benchmarking Data
iLevel	Portfolio Monitoring
Kroll	Portfolio Monitoring, Valuation
Solovis	Portfolio Monitoring

Source: Compiled from various provider websites and tool comparisons.

[a] This list comprises a selection of high-level solutions relevant to the scope of this publication, based on information available from the solution providers' websites and other online resources as of the time of writing. Please note that some specific features or solutions may not be included due to the breadth of offerings in the industry and the dynamic nature of technology.

Table 5.4   Software Solutions Providers (Back Office)

System/Provider Name	High Level Solutions[a]
Carta	Cap Table Management, Valuations, Reporting
FIS Investran	Fund Accounting and Reporting
LemonEdge	Fund Accounting and Reporting
Qashqade	Distribution Waterfall, Carry Calculation

Source: Compiled from various provider websites and tool comparisons.

[a] This list comprises a selection of high-level solutions relevant to the scope of this publication, based on information available from the solution providers' websites and other online resources as of the time of writing. Please note that some specific features or solutions may not be included due to the breadth of offerings in the industry and the dynamic nature of technology.

outstanding in the management of investor relations but might not be easy to integrate with other systems. While a deal-flow system can have all the functionalities needed to effectively handle the deal pipeline, it might not support the particular access control permissions that an alternative investment firm is interested in. Integrated products, despite offering a range of modules, may not exhibit uniform strength across all areas. Initially, these products were developed with a focus on specific operational areas – be it the front, middle, or back office – and over time, they expanded to provide a more comprehensive suite of services. As a result, they tend to excel in the areas where they originated, while the additional functionalities they've added may not be as robust in comparison. While some systems offer analytics capabilities, they may not be as real-time or comprehensive as required.

So, do these best-of-breed and integrated systems solve everything? The simple answer is no; no single system can solve every problem faced by alternative investment firms. Given the wide range of investment strategies and operational frameworks within this industry, firms typically need a blend of systems and services to fully cater to their requirements. In this "hybrid"

Table 5.5 Software Solutions Providers (End-to-End)

System/Provider Name	High Level Solutions[a]
Allvue	Fund Accounting, Investor and Investment Management, Investor Portal, Portfolio Monitoring, Pipeline Management, Compliance
Asset Class	CRM, Investor and Fund Management, Deal and Portfolio Management
Backstop Solutions	CRM, LP Portal/Virtual Data Room, Fundraising, Investor Relations, Portfolio Monitoring
Davigold	CRM, Deal-Flow Management, Portfolio Monitoring, Fund Administration, Investor Relations, ESG and Compliance
Dynamo Software	CRM, Deal Management, Investor Relations, Portfolio Monitoring, Valuation, Fund Accounting, Investor Portal
eFront	CRM, Deal Flow, Fundraising, Fund Administration and Accounting, Portfolio Monitoring, Investor Relations, LP Portal/Virtual Data Room
PE Front Office	CRM, Deal Flow, Investment Management, Fundraising, Fund Management, Portfolio Monitoring, Investor Relations, Investor Portal

Source: Compiled from various provider websites and tool comparisons.

[a] This list comprises a selection of high-level solutions relevant to the scope of this publication, based on information available from the solution providers' websites and other online resources as of the time of writing. Please note that some specific features or solutions may not be included due to the breadth of offerings in the industry and the dynamic nature of technology.

approach the key is in finding the right mix of core systems and complementary tools, ensuring they work in harmony to support the firm's objectives. For example, using this approach an alternative investment firm could deploy a core single integrated system to handle all the core functions of the business, but use best-of-breed solutions for the more complex and unique aspects of their business say carry calculations or waterfall calculations. Another approach is bespoke software development, that is, customization to enhance the functionality of an existing system – and that's covered in the next section.

5.4 Customize the Software or Tweak the Business Process?

Many alternative investment firms have unique investment thesis or operational workflows that their business users are used to. There is no single legal structure associated with alternative investment funds and there could be variations based on jurisdiction, investor type, or industry. Behind the relatively simple-looking high-level model there could be various complex investment models. While there are so many products available, integrated as well as best-of-breed, and they offer standardization, but they do not align perfectly with an alternative investment firm's needs. In such situations, the dilemma arises: should the firm customize the software or adjust its business processes? A crucial strategic choice to be made when integrating technology into the operations of an alternative investment firm is whether to modify business process or customize software. Each choice has its own set of benefits, challenges, and implications for the firm's operational efficiency and adaptability.

Alternative investment firms can adapt existing systems to their own investing strategies and processes through customization. Customization can handle specific requirements related to regulatory compliance, unique asset classes, or workflows that standard software might not be able to handle. This way a customized software can potentially offer a competitive advantage to the firm. Customization does, however, entail costs and risks. It can be costly and time-consuming, frequently needing the help of specialists. In the future, such a customized solution can lead to complications during updating the software and integrations and prolong implementation periods. Moreover, over-customized systems that are too well integrated the current processes become a liability when the market or company strategy changes.

On the other hand, adjusting business processes to conform with standard software functionality can result in improved operations efficiency and cost savings. Using the best practices, which are typically built into the commercial software, this approach capitalizes on provider's experience, knowledge, and product roadmap. With growth of the firm, scalability can also be enhanced through change of business processes. Standardized systems can usually interface with other technologies more conveniently and are generally more upgradeable. However, this approach would require a significant restructuring of the current workflow which is likely to disrupt operations and may be met with resistance from business users that have been using the same process.

The decision as to whether modify the software or adjust the business process is about considering the long-term strategic benefits of each option. Alternative investment firms must consider their size and future expansion and make a choice that aligns with their strategic objectives, operational needs, and resource constraints. Standard systems with flexible processes could be more suited for very small firms or with very fast growth, while customizable solutions are more advantageous for medium or large firms with well-established workflows. The selection will also be influenced by the firm's operational complexity and investment strategy. Alternative investment firms may have unique or specialized investment strategies and automation of those may typically require custom-made tools in order to effectively monitor and report on assets. Regulatory environment is another major consideration before a software can be selected and implemented within an alternative investment firm. Customization might be needed in firms that are operating in jurisdictions that have very specific or rigid regulatory needs to attain compliance. Hence, it is necessary for organizations to evaluate their current needs and future objectives, weighing the advantages that industry-standard processes have versus the total cost of ownership of custom solutions. Finally, the selected strategy should help the company to remain competitive and be flexible enough to cope with the changes in the market or the technology in the future.

5.5 Summary

The alternative investment technology world is rather crowded with systems and services, which are designed to help different stages and aspects of the investment lifecycle. However, there is no one-size-fits-all solution that would be in line with the strategic plans and vision of an alternative investment firm and at the same time help in reaching the necessary operational efficiency. Firms must choose between integrated systems, which may not be the best in every category, but cover several functions, and specialized systems that excel in certain areas but are difficult to integrate. The size of an organization, cost constraints, IT competences, scalability, data consistency, usability, and strategic vision determine the choice between an integrated solution and a number of small systems. Customization of software makes it possible to adapt the software to individual business processes; however, it is usually costly and complicated. On the other hand, customizing business processes to standardized software can lead to cost reduction and best practices adoption, but this may require substantial organizational change management.

The process of selecting technology services and solutions should be iterative and aligned with the alternative investment firm's strategic vision. The technology dilemma is not an IT-driven project to make one of the simple choices but rather a complex balancing act. The key lies in making informed, strategic decisions that not only address current dilemmas but also lead the way for future success and adaptability in an ever-changing market.

Chapter 6

Technology Dilemma 3: Where to Run the Systems?

6.1   Introduction

Technology that changed in every respect during the last two decades has forced every business to reassess their technology infrastructures. Even the alternative investment firms do not remain unaffected from this digital revolution onset and its related subtleties. This chapter deals with the dilemma of the alternative investment industry players as to where to deploy the systems, that is, the dilemma of choosing where to run their systems.

Choosing the right infrastructure is critical as it not only becomes the operational backbone of the firm but also makes it scalable, efficient, and flexible. This also has far-reaching consequences for regulatory compliance and investor trust. Choosing between cloud-based Software as a Service (SaaS) or

DOI: 10.1201/9781003481652-6

traditional on-premises solutions is not only a technical decision but also a strategic one. This infrastructure dilemma is further compounded by other factors such as cost, security, scalability, and operation resilience.

6.2   SaaS or On-Premises Solutions?

The debate between cloud-based SaaS and on-premises solutions is not new and with every passing year it is getting more and more tilted in favor of SaaS. And it is not just an academic discussion; it affects the bottom line of firms. According to a 2022 report by Gartner, the SaaS market grew by 17.4%, indicating a strong trend toward cloud-based solutions. For alternative investments, this trend is exemplified by the increase in adoption of SaaS products by asset managers seeking to benefit from specialized tools ranging from real-time data analysis to investment management.

With the surge in data volumes and the need for real-time analytics, firms face the critical decision of where to host their operational systems – cloud or on-premises? It might seem straightforward, but it's useful to briefly examine the actual definitions of these terms. Cloud computing delivers services like data storage, servers, and software over the internet. Traditionally, on-premises computing involves data and application management on physical infrastructure within an organization's location. The primary distinction used to be the location of infrastructure; however, now it often revolves around ownership. Nowadays, companies can host their servers in the cloud yet manage them directly, blurring the traditional lines between cloud and on-premises models by shifting focus to server ownership. In Figure 6.1, Gartner says that over the next few years, cloud computing will continue to evolve from being an innovation facilitator to a business disruptor and, ultimately, a business necessity.

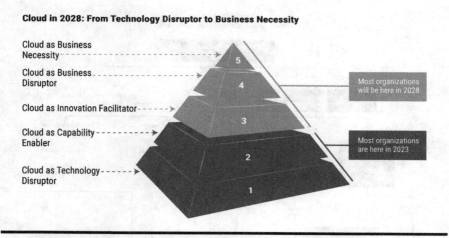

Cloud in 2028: From Technology Disruptor to Business Necessity

Cloud as Business Necessity

Cloud as Business Disruptor

Cloud as Innovation Facilitator

Cloud as Capability Enabler

Cloud as Technology Disruptor

Most organizations will be here in 2028

Most organizations are here in 2023

Figure 6.1   The Future of Cloud Computing through 2028.

Applications can be deployed and run in both the models – cloud as well as on-premises. SaaS is a model where software applications are delivered over the internet, allowing users to access and use the software without managing the underlying infrastructure. This model provides flexibility, scalability, accessibility, and cost-efficiency (upfront as well as ongoing), as it typically operates on a subscription basis. On-premises solutions, in contrast, involve installing and running software on physical servers either located within an organization's premises or located on cloud but under organization's ownership. This gives businesses complete control over their data and security and offers more customization capability but requires higher upfront capital expenditure and more resources for management and maintenance. The decision between SaaS and on-premises models is based on several factors such as cost and investment, accessibility, and management overhead and Figure 6.2 helps make the decision based on these factors.

To elaborate a little more, Figure 6.2 helps firms on taking a decision based on initial and ongoing expenses versus long-term capital investment, accessibility just within the office or

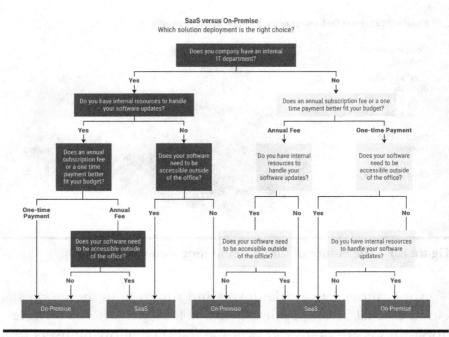

Figure 6.2   SaaS versus On-Premises – Making the Right Choice.

even from outside, and the capability to manage IT inhouse.
But this decision is not just about selecting the most cost-
effective or accessible solution; it's also linked to complex
regulatory compliance requirements, such as mandates for
data to reside within the country of operation. When it comes
to the alternative investment sector, which includes assets
like hedge funds, private equity, and real estate, regulatory
compliance becomes even more nuanced and critical due to
the complex and often opaque nature of these investments.
Standardized compliance certifications (such ISO 27001 and
SOC 2) are usually provided by SaaS providers and may meet
broad criteria. On-premises solutions, however, might give
companies with extremely specific compliance requirements
more freedom to customize security measures and audit
procedures.

The alternative investments industry is global in operations, but firms must adhere to local data residency regulations in the regions that operate or raise capital. Firms who deal with EU investors, for example, must comply with General Data Protection Regulation (GDPR), which means they have to assess if SaaS providers can handle and store data within specific regions or if on-premises solutions are required to be compliant. Depending on investor base, fund structure, and investment strategy, alternative investment firms are subject to various regulations. Strict reporting and transparency requirements are set by the regulation such as the Alternative Investment Fund Managers Directive (AIFMD) in Europe, and this has an effect on the firms' decisions on how they select and implement IT solutions for data management and reporting. The alternative investing firms are required to have comprehensive audit trails to satisfy the investors and regulators. Firms must be satisfied that the on-premises or SaaS IT system they choose offers tamperproof, complete records of investor communications, transactional data, and decision-making processes. International data transfer regulations are especially important because alternative investing firms often operate cross-border. The complexity of compliance in data transfers between jurisdictions may influence businesses consider on-premises solutions, which provide them with more control over the data storage and transfer processes. Another trend is the adoption of hybrid cloud solutions, which provide the flexibility and scalability of the cloud with the control and security of on-premises infrastructure. With this approach, organizations can comply with regulatory requirements by storing sensitive data on-premises and using cloud for low-sensitive operations, for example, an alternative investment firm may decide to store sensitive investor information on-premises and use cloud-based analytics and processing capabilities for market data and investment research.

6.3 How Critical Is Business Continuity via Systems?

It is an era where technology and information systems define the operational backbone of businesses across industries and thus business continuity through robust technology and systems is of critical significance. The alternative investment sector is not immune to operational disruptions caused by natural disasters, cyberattacks, or technological failures. System uptime is essential in the world of alternative investments where decisions are time sensitive. The significance of robustness and accessibility in systems was highlighted by the COVID-19 pandemic.

Having an effective and watertight business continuity plan (BCP) and disaster recovery (DR) plan is not only about technology uptime but has implications for organizational resilience, stakeholder trust, and regulatory compliance. Systems play a defining role in firm's resilience, that is, its ability to anticipate, prepare for, respond to, and recover from changes and sudden disruptions. An effective business continuity strategy ensures that critical business functions remain available and reliable in the face of disruptions, thereby safeguarding operational integrity and continuity. The trust of stakeholders, including suppliers, investors, employees, and investee companies, is directly influenced by the reliability of business processes. A firm's ability to maintain continuity through resilient systems demonstrates a commitment to stakeholder needs and instills trust and confidence. Like other industries, even in alternative investments, regulatory frameworks mandate stringent business continuity and DR plans. For example, regulations such as GDPR impose obligations on firms to ensure the availability and integrity of critical systems and protect sensitive information under all circumstances. Non-compliance may not only lead to fines and legal complications but can cause reputational damage too.

Technology infrastructure and system deployment options play an enormous role in business continuity and DR planning. During COVID-19 pandemic firms who relied on on-premises systems experienced difficulties while those that relied on cloud-based systems could seamlessly transition to remote work. There are a few organizations (e.g., Business Continuity Institute, Uptime Institute) who do periodic surveys, studies, and research on the topics of operational resilience and infrastructure availability. There is an indirect correlation that businesses with cloud services experience 35% less downtime and operational disruption compared to those with primarily on-site IT resources. Due to their distributed design good SaaS solutions can provide robust DR and business continuity benefits. SaaS solutions often include robust DR capabilities as part of the service itself, potentially offering better business continuity with less effort from the business itself. Evaluating the Recovery Time Objective (RTO) and Recovery Point Objective (RPO) should be a key criterion in the critical assessment when choosing a SaaS solution. On-premises systems may offer a sense of control but require significant investment in redundancy and DR planning and implementing business continuity strategy. Even if the deployment model chosen by a firm is on-premises it can always utilize cloud technology to implement BCPs – leading to a kind of hybrid model again. The flexibility, scalability, and affordability of cloud platforms make them perfect for DR and data backup solutions. Using cloud services, businesses may replicate vital information and applications across multiple data centers, ensuring availability even in the event of a disaster affecting one site. Furthermore, because the cloud's pay-as-you-go model removes the need for a significant initial investment in physical equipment, firms of all sizes may now afford to implement robust continuity planning.

6.4 Security Challenges (Cloud vs On-Premises)

Security is a concern for any system and a paramount concern for alternative investment firms and their financial systems given the sensitive nature of financial data. Maintaining security and safety of investor's information and investment details is crucial for trust building in the world of alternative investments. Investment firms' systems must be really robust to counter more frequent and smarter data breaches, unauthorized access, and cyber threats. If these details are stolen or revealed publicly, it can severely tarnish a company's reputation, diminish trust among investors as well as result in financial hardships and legal challenges.

Whether an alternative investment firm chooses cloud-based services (SaaS) or on-premises applications security is a non-negotiable factor. Cloud solutions are managed by the service providers and ensuring security is their responsibility; however, in the case of on-premises deployments, the burden of securing the infrastructure falls entirely on the alternative investment firm. Cloud service providers (CSPs) can often invest more in security resources than individual firms. The cloud services have made a considerable progress, having many companies like Amazon Web Services and Microsoft Azure pumping a vast sum of money annually for the security of the cloud services. The cloud's ability to provide advanced encryption, threat detection, and compliance with the standards like ISO 27001 has enabled the firms to have strong security features. Nevertheless, attacks such as the one experienced in the 2020 SolarWinds cyberattack that impacted numerous financial entities is an indication that the threats are ever present, therefore, emphasizing the importance of robust security policies across any chosen infrastructure. In the cloud, data is stored off-site and typically across multiple locations, raising issues of data security and privacy. Alternative investment firms need to make sure that cloud service providers (CSPs) use strong encryption and data protection methods, meeting the standards of regulations like GDPR, AIFMD, and others. The cloud management of sensitive data access is critical. There should be a capability for firms to be able to create and impose strict access policies and only authorized people should be able to access the critical information. Alternative investment firms should comply with the multiple financial regulations that may involve some special requirements relating to cloud services hosting and processing.

The on-premises solutions provide companies full control over their data and systems, but they also come with their own set of security challenges. Operation of an on-premises infrastructure comes at a high price of building and securing physical infrastructure and hardware environment along with having dedicated IT staff. Firms are accountable for all systems being up-to-date and ensuring this will be a struggle as threat landscape changes. Scaling security with an on-premises solution can turn out to be costly and slow, and eventually lead to the appearance of time frames where the environment becomes vulnerable while the transition is underway.

To solve those challenges, alternative investment firms should implement the security best practices regardless of if they go for cloud or on-premises solutions. Firms should undertake periodic security audits to identify vulnerabilities and act accordingly. The data should be encrypted in transit and at rest with mechanisms for protection of sensitive data. Firms should enforce tight access management rules and use multi-factor authentication to ensure that only authorized users have permissions to systems. They need to create a compliance strategy that aligns with both industry regulations and its own specific operational standards. However, last but not the least, firms should have a well-documented incident response plan so as to act quickly when any security incidents occur.

6.5 Summary

The choice of the location for the system running in the alternative investment sector depends on many factors and there is no direct answer to it. It calls for a considerate evaluation of the needs and capabilities of the firm in terms of the advantages and disadvantages of each system deployment option. The choice must correspond to the strategic objectives of the company, operational abilities, and the industry regulations. Even though the cloud delivers scalability and saving, the on-premises solutions provide the sense of governance and data proximity. Alternative investment firms must align their infrastructure plan with their business strategy while considering their risk profile and unique operations. This decision will define the operational competences and strategic direction of alternative investment firms, as technology evolves.

BCP is vital in ensuring that operations continue without major disruptions when there is failure of system or disaster strikes. The multi-faceted business continuity achieved via system brings organizational resilience, stakeholder trust, regulatory compliance, and competitive advantage. Sound business continuity and DR investments are not only risk-mitigation activities but also more of a critical strategic enabler that is critical for a long-term viability and success of a firm. Hence business system resilience is the key ingredient of the modern business model for overcoming the challenges of the current times.

The decision between cloud and on-premises solutions is critical for alternative investment firms, with each option bringing a distinct set of security challenges that need to be weighed against the firm's needs and the applicable regulatory requirements. For firms, the sensitivity of their data, the regulatory environment, and their ability to manage security internally must be taken into account. Having best practice and a security plan enable firms to face these challenges and determine the right IT infrastructure for their business operations and their investors' interest.

Bibliography

Gartner Research on Market Share: Enterprise Application Software as a Service, Worldwide, 2022 (www.gartner.com/en/documents/4466999).

The BCI – Global membership association for business continuity and resilience professionals (www.thebci.org/).

Uptime Institute –- advisory organization focused on improving the performance, efficiency, and reliability of business critical infrastructure (https://uptimeinstitute.com/).

Chapter 7

Technology Dilemma 4: Is Automation Worth the Cost?

7.1 Introduction

Today, using technology is an essential part of the alternative investment business operations. The deal management, investor communication, investment management, trade execution, as well as compliance functions, to name but a few, leverage in a significant way software and automation. For alternative investing organizations, the introduction of cutting-edge technologies has brought with it both tremendous opportunities and formidable challenges. The dependence on technology brings a lot of benefits – better efficiency, reduced costs, quicker processes, more robust risk management, and data-driven decision-making with analytics.

However, new technology implementation also calls for significant investment of money as well as time. Licensed

DOI: 10.1201/9781003481652-7

software, hardware upgrades, IT staff, and consultants to implement and manage systems can be a considerable expense. Customizing technology solutions to specific needs of alternative investment firm and ensuring scalability can add to expenses. Further, integrating new systems with legacy or existing systems and processes is often complex and disruptive. Due to narrow margins and fee pressure in the alternative investment industry, business leaders are facing hard decisions about what technology initiatives to fund with the scarce capital at their disposal.

This current chapter explores the dilemma that alternative investment firms experience regarding technology spending and then analyzes the costs versus potential value of automation, evaluate build versus buy decisions for IT systems, and discuss how to achieve the right balance of technology investment to gain competitive advantage while maintaining the return ratios that measure the performance of the managed funds.

7.2   Cost versus Value

Spending on new technology always requires a cost-benefit analysis and it becomes the cornerstone of the decision-making process for alternative investment firms. Initially, the investment required for implementing new information systems or technologies can be substantial, encompassing not only the direct costs of software and hardware but also the ancillary expenses related to IT staff, training, consultants, data migration, and integration services. Leaders of the firm always ask themselves – will this investment in automation provide value greater than the cost, that is, will there be a significant return on investment (ROI)? Predicting ROI is difficult as the true value of technology is often indirect and realized over time, not immediately. However, to understand or measure the value side of the equation, it is helpful to consider some of the key ways technology can improve operations:

- **Efficiency Gains:** Automation of manual processes like data entry and report generation removes tedious work and allows staff to focus on higher-value tasks. This can significantly increase productivity. Everyone looks at the same data, that is, single source of truth which takes accuracy also to a different level. The reputational damage and loss of investor trust caused by inaccurate data or reporting failures is immense and can threaten an investment firm's future viability. The value of preventable data errors is therefore immeasurable.
- **Better Decision-Making:** Advanced data analytics and AI-driven insights enable more informed and timely investment decisions. Technology can surface trends, signals, and predictive analytics that humans could miss. Automation opens the door to innovative investment strategies and analytical models, offering firms a competitive edge in a market that values agility and insight.
- **Risk Reduction:** Automated compliance checks, portfolio monitoring, and accurate reporting can systematically reduce different types of risk especially those related to human error. This protects the business from non-compliance penalties and potential financial losses. Investing in compliance technologies helps prevent much costlier regulatory fines, lawsuits, and reputational damage that non-compliance can bring.
- **Improved Investor Service:** Investor portals, digital document management, and customer relationship management (CRM) systems create a better investor experience. Investors today expect more than just competitive financial returns – they demand a service experience from investment firms that is seamless, personalized, and accessible across channels. They

also demand greater transparency and insight into their investments. As technology builds trust and confidence with investors through secure, seamless experiences, it becomes a strategic asset worth the cost.

▪ **Future Scalability:** Technology creates capacity to handle increasing operational volume without linearly increasing headcount and is a major cost advantage. It creates economies of scale and enables firms to improve returns. Good technology solutions allow small teams to manage large and fast-growing portfolios of assets and investors.

Costs for having good technology systems can vary from few thousand dollars annually to even millions of dollars for some alternative investment firms. It depends on the size of firm, number of users, and current state of automation within the firm. But for certain business critical systems, the expense is justified many times over by the value added in the ways described above. Leaders of the firm should carefully analyze the costs and benefits of any potential technology investment based on their specific strategic needs and objectives. They must also keep in consideration that new systems must integrate with existing infrastructure and processes to fully realize value. Lack of integration can limit benefits hence measuring value of a system running in silo will not be fair. Technology evolves quickly so today's investments may become obsolete faster than expected. This shortens the useful lifecycle hence all projects should be time bound and must be given sufficient time to explore full benefits of the system. The increasing use of technology brings cybersecurity risks, which can lead to potential losses, offsetting the value gained from technological advancements hence along with any new system its security measures should be part of the project itself. A thorough cost-benefit analysis, including a detailed assessment of both direct and indirect costs versus the tangible and intangible benefits, is essential. While disciplined diligence is required, the long-term value enabled by the right technology choices will typically outweigh the initial price tag. Some firms may also choose a phased technology implementation strategy to spread out costs and evaluate the value at each stage.

Gareth Richardson, Chief Operating Officer at Thought Machine, Advisor & Non-executive Director, accurately describes the gradual but impactful nature of technology automation, stating,

> Technology automation is not a sprint, it is an overarching philosophy, it requires time to mature and its true value in enhancing productivity to be realized. Initial efforts may seem modest, results not immediately visible and the temptation to use manual approaches seem compelling; but with time, the systems mature, efficiency evolves, and its value manifests and becomes obvious.

7.3 Inhouse IT Team or Outsourced – What Is the Right Balance?

Alternative investment firms change a lot as they grow from their first fund to say seventh or eighth fund – they become more procedure oriented, larger teams, tons of data, and trying to adhere to more regulatory standards and adopt best practices. Hence their IT needs also change as they grow. Because the transition from first fund to subsequent funds rarely goes as planned, the IT capabilities need to be just as nimble as the rest of their operations. Figure 7.1 shows there could be some rough guidelines for building IT capabilities as an alternate investment firm moves from one fund to the next. Considering a traditional growth scenario the first fund is often the leanest and most firms choose to outsource all their IT needs. By the second or third fund a CFO is brough abord who often doubles as the head of IT and managing IT becomes a

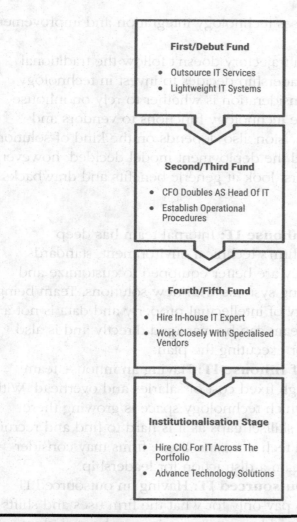

Figure 7.1 Growth of IT Capabilities within an Alternative Investment Firm.

common function for the CFO. At some point, the firm's internal staff grows to a size that requires someone inhouse to manage the IT on a daily basis. The next stage is appointing a full-fledged Chief Information Officer who not only manages IT for the firm but addresses technology integration and improvement across the portfolio.

Since the growth trajectory doesn't follow the traditional path hence once leadership decides to invest in technology initiatives, a key consideration is whether to rely on inhouse IT staff or outsource technology functions to vendors and consultants. The decision also depends on the kind of solutions being looked at and the deployment model decided; however, it's worthwhile to first look at generic benefits and drawbacks to each approach:

- **Benefits of Inhouse IT:** Internal team has deep knowledge of firm's technical environment, standards, and needs. They are better equipped to customize and integrate existing systems with new solutions. Team being internal security of intellectual property and data is not a big concern. Team can be managed directly and is also accountable for executing the plan.
- **Drawbacks of Inhouse IT:** Having an inhouse team translates to high fixed cost of salaries and overhead. With the speed at which technology space is growing there will always be skillset gaps as it is hard to find and recruit expertise in all tech domains. Some firms may consider managing IT team a distraction for leadership.
- **Benefits of Outsourced IT:** Having an outsourced IT team allows to pay only for what the firm uses and shifts fixed cost to variable cost. Team size can be scaled up or down as needed. In this model firm can have access to specialized skills which are otherwise difficult to hire. Leaders don't have to manage the outsourced team and hence can focus on the core business.
- **Drawbacks of Outsourced IT:** External team has less familiarity with firm's technical environment, standards, and needs. Team being external security of intellectual property and data confidentiality is a big concern. There will always

be lack of direct oversight. While the team doesn't need to be managed directly, vendor management can still consume some time and energy.

For any alternative investment firm, it's not going to be an easy answer because neither of the approaches is without risks or concerns. Commodity functions like email, cloud storage, and end-user tech support can be safely outsourced to vendors to gain efficiency and majority of the firms do this irrespective of their size. Tricky part is core competencies that differentiate the investment firm, like proprietary investment models, profit-sharing models, or carry calculations, that firms prefer to maintain control and security on. Big firms, having a lot of such proprietary information, typically prefer to develop their own bespoke inhouse solutions which has its own challenges in the long run. However, for majority of other firms, choice would be to keep the models inhouse and feed the output from them in the systems they subscribe to. This hybrid approach allows keeping the core competencies that differentiate the investment firm to be managed internally while leveraging vendor solutions for technology expertise.

There could be another flavor of hybrid model where there is no proprietary knowledge involved, for example, implementing a CRM system or data warehouse. Such technology initiatives could also benefit from a blended model where internal IT staff who understand the firm's environment and requirements can lead the project management and decision-making while external consultants can supplement with specialized technical skills to execute the implementation.

The right balance depends on the firm's existing capabilities and staff expertise. Having an inhouse IT expert will not ensure a flawless performance but it can remove the waiting time. Value of someone on the inside is continuity. Non-core functions can be safely outsourced if quality vendors are available. Business leaders must carefully analyze their specific environment and needs when choosing the optimal sources of technological capabilities.

7.4 Seamless Support for Systems – It's Beyond Price and Compliance

Once systems are in place, ongoing management and support is crucial for technology to deliver lasting value. Implementing new technologies offers little value without seamless support for ongoing operations and maintenance. While the capabilities of the software or platform itself are crucial, the behind-the-scenes services keeping systems running are the true foundation for delivering business value. Support is not just an add-on element or box to check – it is integral to unlocking the return on investment from technology. Seamless systems support provides uninterrupted, timely, and comprehensive assistance for users of implemented technologies. The goal is minimizing disruptions and issues, so users can be maximally productive leveraging the systems. Technology support generally falls into two main categories that work together to enable business value:

7.4.1 Front-End User Support

This involves providing resources and assistance directly to employees, customers, and other end users of technology systems. Areas encompassed in front-end support include:

- Training users on new software platforms and features
- IT help desk for answering user questions
- How-to documentation, user manuals, and knowledge bases
- Troubleshooting issues experienced by end users
- Assisting with user adoption and change management
- Gathering feedback to improve user experience

The goal is for end users to leverage technology easily and independently to be productive. Effective front-end support delivers the capabilities users need when they need them.

7.4.2   Back-End Infrastructure Support

This includes the technical personnel, tools, and processes required to keep infrastructure operational behind the scenes. Key aspects include:

- Monitoring performance metrics 24/7 and responding to alerts
- Managing backups, redundancy, failover systems, and business continuity protections
- Performing regular maintenance like hardware refreshes, software patches, OS upgrades
- Continuously detecting and resolving potential vulnerabilities
- Conducting disaster recovery testing and simulations
- Monitoring security threats and defending against attacks

Strong infrastructure support ensures all front-end systems have the back-end stability, availability and data protection required to minimize disruptions. Smooth back-end operations enable seamless user experiences.

In the case of on-premises solution, both the support types are critical; however, if an alternative investment firm decides to subscribe to SaaS solutions, then back-end infrastructure support is handled by the vendor providing the SaaS. Evaluation of SaaS providers should definitely consider some key factors especially for critical business systems.

When downtime equates to lost productivity, having confidence in a SaaS vendor's ability to provide quick resolutions with knowledgeable staff is critical. As covered in Table 7.1, alternative investment firm must evaluate each

Table 7.1 Vendor Evaluation Criteria on Support Options

Evaluation Criteria	Details to Look For
Support Channels	What options are available to obtain support – phone, email, live chat, online knowledge base? Are there offerings like 24/7 or premium support?
Support Hours	What are the coverage windows and time zones? Is after-hours or weekend support included?
Support SLAs	Are service level agreements provided defining response times and resolutions for issues of varying severity?
Uptime Guarantee	Does the vendor guarantee a certain percentage of uptime per month/year? Any credits provided for any failures to meet the SLA?
Domain Expertise	Does the provider have seasoned staff with expertise in alternative investment industry and business needs? Do they understand niche domain requirements?

Source: Author.

vendor's historical uptime record and the breadth of support options. For business-critical apps, premium support levels and guaranteed Service Level Agreements (SLAs) provide peace of mind worth the added cost. The goal is to minimize business disruptions and maximize productivity.

Irrespective of the deployment model (SaaS or on-premises) another very effective strategy when rolling out new software, systems, or technologies across an alternative investment firm is assigning product champions across different functions. Product champions are power users who spearhead adoption within their business unit. Their responsibilities typically include:

■ Attending specialized training on the technology first.
■ Learning the system in depth so they become a local expert.

- Communicating updates, changes, and new features to their business unit.
- Providing first-level support to peers on usage questions.
- Gathering feedback from users to share with IT/ implementation teams.
- Promoting adoption and enthusiasm for the system.
- Role modeling best practices for workflows.

Having product champions and their support streamlines IT teams' efforts. With this model, the support function is distributed across units instead of IT team being the sole support hub. With engaged and informed users evangelizing the system from within each business unit, support needs are addressed quickly. Meanwhile IT staff can focus on enhancing and optimizing for long-term success. Product champions are a "train the trainer" approach that scales support for smooth organizational adoption. Their insights provide user feedback to guide ongoing enhancements as well. With concerted outreach across the organization, they pave the way for a successful technology launch.

A very essential component in providing effective support is a support tracking system for monitoring, coordinating, and continuously improving technology support across an alternative investment firm. This could be an inhouse solution or can be chosen from plethora of choices available as SaaS products. Each SaaS provider will have their own support tracking system; however, rather than tracking tickets on multiple systems, it's essential for alternative investment firm to have a central knowledge base of known issues and fixes. An effective issue tracking system should include ticket workflows assigning issues to appropriate IT specialists, categorization by system module, error type, user segment, etc., priority levels, notifications, and dashboards for tracking trends. Issue tracking and structured workflow processes facilitate superior support delivery, issue prevention, and continuous optimization, across the technology landscape. The behind the scenes oversight and management capabilities of an issue tracking system is what ensures seamless user experiences.

Implementation of technology and efficiency capabilities usually involves substantial investment, which is more than just obtaining the core software. It involves people, processes, and technologies that are dedicated to maintaining the availability and consistent performance of systems. Costs of ongoing support should be factored in technology initiatives. The price tag may seem a bit high initially, but the costs of instability are higher. New systems' initial costs and ongoing support and compliance costs should be considered jointly in evaluating technology investments. Summing the efficiency gains, risk reduction, and potential growth enabled, and comparing them with the costs, will result in decisions which maximize return on technology investments while maintaining the firms stable and compliant.

7.5 Summary

Technology allows other investment firms to improve performance, fortify risk management, and speed up growth in ways that would not be feasible otherwise. It is an essential facilitator in various business critical functions. However, in assessing investments of technology solutions, alternative investment firms are presented with the challenge of balancing tangible costs with long-term strategic value that is difficult to quantify. The choice of technology investments is not only a question of money but also operational and strategic decision which can significantly determine the growth and scalability of the company.

The value of technology investments can be maximized by alternative investment firms with the help of value potential analysis, using hybrid IT teams, and seamless systems support.

With diligent management, technology can improve efficiency and functioning to yield better returns. To navigate the cost versus value dilemma, firms may use different approaches, such as pilot programs, partnerships with fintech companies, or incremental investments in emerging technologies. With these approaches, firms can a test a technology without upfront substantial resource expenditure; hence, dampening the risk and offering a more informed analysis of the technology's value proposition.

Chapter 8

Technology Dilemma 5: How to Access the Systems?

8.1   Introduction

In an era where financial markets operate on a global scale and around the clock, the ability to access systems and data anywhere and anytime has become a critical component of the alternative investment industry. Access to systems has a direct role in the operational efficiency and data security of alternative investment firms. With more capabilities moving to the cloud and a remote or hybrid workforce demanding flexibility, firms are evaluating access approaches balancing usability and security. Employees need mobile access from multiple devices, external partners require selective access, and cyber threats necessitate stringent authentication safeguards.

Navigating these access requirements poses challenges and risks. While cloud computing and mobile technology allow

DOI: 10.1201/9781003481652-8

for unprecedented flexibility, overly restrictive access hampers productivity. Flexibility introduces significant security risks and breaches via compromised credentials or devices lead to data loss, compliance violations and reputational damage. For example, as per the industry surveys by CyberEdge Group in 2022 and 2023 security posture of respondent organizations highlight the IT domain that most concerns them is mobile devices such as smartphones and tablets. These surveys clearly show that IT security teams continue to be nervous about securing employee-owned mobile devices. Firms must outline policies governing access standards across systems and data classifications. Then processes like identity management and device management can enforce proper controls.

This chapter delves into the critical dilemma of balancing the need for secure and efficient access to technological systems within alternative investment firms and examines leading practices for governing, enabling, and securing system access. It discusses considerations for company-managed versus personal devices, evaluate access limitations balancing confidentiality with practicality, and present models to provide external partner access. Recommendations are grounded in standards like NIST and ISO that are applicable to any organization, regardless of its size or industry, including the alternative investment industry. By proactively addressing system access, alternative firms can enable both security and productivity.

8.2   Enterprise Devices or Bring Your Own Device

The debate between the adoption of enterprise devices versus Bring Your Own Device (BYOD) policies has been there all the while. Historically, alternative firms issued corporate devices to retain control over security and access. But preferences for flexibility are driving BYOD adoption. While company-managed devices simplify security protocols, employees prefer using their personal devices. During and after COVID-19, supporting a remote workforce is a necessary requirement. Firms now face a decision between maintaining tight control through enterprise device policies versus enabling productivity with BYOD models.

When deciding between enterprise devices and a BYOD policy, firms must weigh several factors; however, it's worthwhile to examine the pros and cons of each model or approach.

- **Pros of Company-Provided Devices Model:**
  Enterprise devices allow firms standardize and maintain strict control over hardware and software configurations thus simplifying security management. Since a standard model is followed, support is also streamlined. If needed devices can be locked down more strictly. All data of the firm remains on its own devices. A 2020 study by IBM found that enterprise device users reported fewer instances of unauthorized data access.
- **Cons of Company-Provided Devices Model:**
  Due to hardware and software policy restrictions, employees may need to manage separate personal and work devices. Remote wipe policies raise privacy concerns and risk to personal data on work devices. If all devices are provided by the firm, then it's a higher capital expenditure.
- **Pros of BYOD Model:**
  BYOD policy empowers employees with the choice to use their personal devices for work. This flexibility can lead to increased employee satisfaction and productivity. It saves the firm from capital expenditure of procuring and refreshing devices.
- **Cons of BYOD Model:**
  Use of personal devices under BYOD policy introduce a variety of security challenges. The diversity of devices and operating systems introduces complexities in maintaining

uniform security safeguards. Firms have privacy concerns around any official data on the devices.

In a survey by Bitglass (now a Forcepoint company), 69% of companies allow employees to use their personal devices for work purposes to some extent. Additionally, some organizations have extended BYOD policies beyond internal staff to also encompass contractors, partners, customers, and suppliers. Output of the survey, shown in Figure 8.1, revealed significant concerns remain around personal device usage despite growing BYOD adoption. Sixty-three percent of respondents cited data leakage as their top BYOD security worry. Unauthorized data access and malware threats also ranked as primary concerns, at 53% and 52%, respectively. Most organizations are still unprepared to address BYOD risks, even as deployment accelerates.

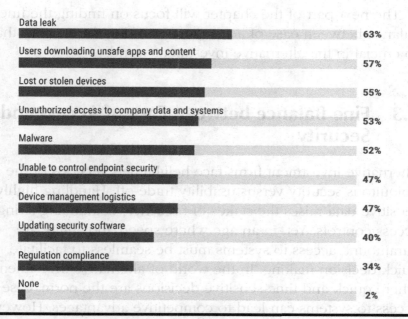

Data leak — 63%
Users downloading unsafe apps and content — 57%
Lost or stolen devices — 55%
Unauthorized access to company data and systems — 53%
Malware — 52%
Unable to control endpoint security — 47%
Device management logistics — 47%
Updating security software — 40%
Regulation compliance — 34%
None — 2%

Figure 8.1   Main Security Concerns Related to BYOD.

Alternative investment firms face a strategic decision between enterprise and BYOD approaches, each with clear trade-offs. Company devices provide security but reduce agility and user experience. BYOD offers flexibility and potential cost savings, yet exponentially heightens security risks requiring investment to manage. For alternative investment firms, where confidentiality and data integrity are paramount, enterprise devices seem to be an obvious choice; however, firms must weigh whether to optimize for security or enable productivity within acceptable risk parameters. In practice, many firms take a hybrid approach – providing corporate laptops but allowing personal smartphones and tablets under strict policy controls. They follow the practice of establishing standardized policies first, then utilizing technologies like mobile device management (MDM) to apply controls. In such an approach, firms provide standard configured laptops with data loss prevention controls and BYOD phones/tablets are enrolled into MDM for selective wipe.

The next part of the chapter will focus on finding the fine balance between ease of access and ensuring the security that is so crucial in the alternative investment world.

8.3 Fine Balance between Ease of Access and Security

Alternative investment firms face heightened versions of the ubiquitous security versus usability trade-off. Handling highly sensitive data raises the stakes of breaches, demanding stringent access controls. Yet, in an age where speed and agility are paramount, access to systems must be seamless to facilitate quick decision-making. In the world of alternative investments, where quick and time-sensitive decisions are the norm, ease of access to systems can lead to competitive advantages. However, each access point can also be a potential vulnerability and hence it's important to balance ease of access with the robust security measures. When defining system and data access policies, alternative investment firms make difficult balancing decisions between security, productivity, and flexibility. Enabling employee mobility generally conflicts with locking down data tightly. Allowing external partner integration conflicts with air-gapped internal controls. Navigating these trade-offs relies on data classifications and layered controls as each data type warrants correlated restrictions.

Convenience is a crucial factor for productivity. A system that is cumbersome to access can hinder timely investments and critical market movements. For BYOD, the convenience is inherent as employees use their own devices and are familiar with them, reducing the learning curve and potentially increasing productivity. Ease of access often comes with security trade-offs. For enterprise devices, the risk lies in the potential for these devices to be lost or stolen, leading to unauthorized access. With BYOD, the risks are multiplied, with varied device security levels and potential for these personal devices to be compromised outside of the firm's secure environment. Before looking at the balancing strategies it would be good to recap some of the security, usability, and data protection considerations.

8.3.1 Usability Considerations

- Single Sign On (SSO), that is, easy login without numerous credentials across apps
- Anytime, anywhere, any device access keeps employees productive remotely
- Self-service password reset avoids help desk bottlenecks

8.3.2 Security Considerations

- Limiting access to information by user type, device types, and restricting actions

- Quick de-provisioning of user access after employee's exit
- Continuous monitoring of user activity to detect suspicious access attempts
- Authenticating identities rigorously with multi-factor authentication (MFA)

8.3.3 Data Protection Considerations

- Classifying data by sensitivity then correlating controls (e.g., watermarks, encryption)
- Controlling any data transfer from user devices
- Controlling copy/paste and local file downloads
- Marking emails/documents with visibility restrictions
- Remote wipe policies for company devices

Some strategies alternative investment firms can employ to balance usability, security, and data protection:

- **Multi-factor Authentication**: MFA adds layers of security, making system access secure even if a device falls into the wrong hands. It provides added identity assurance and according to Microsoft, MFA can prevent 99.9% of account compromise attacks.
- **Endpoint Security Solutions:** It can provide hardened endpoint infrastructure protections including firewalls, antimalware, encryption, and access controls that travel with devices. These can monitor and manage the security of both enterprise and personal devices.
- **Regular and Automated Security Audits:** Regular checks can ensure that all devices comply with the firm's security policies. Continuous automated scans can programmatically inspect systems and code for risks like open ports, unpatched flaws, and misconfigurations. There are tools that can be utilized to automatically submit fixes or alert IT teams.

■ **Employee Training:** Educating employees on security best practices can mitigate risks associated with BYOD. Comprehensive cybersecurity and compliance education can set employee's expectations around access policies, handling sensitive data, and reporting risks or suspicious activity.

Aforementioned strategies can mitigate risks without overly complicating access. However, adoption of these strategies in financial sector varies, especially with smaller firms often lagging behind due to concerns about user reluctance and friction. Moreover, evolving regulatory compliance mandates also influence security and access policies by setting strict standards around data privacy and controls. Frameworks like GDPR in Europe, CCPA in California, and POPIA in South Africa mandate large portions of cybersecurity best practices into compliance requirements with financial penalties for non-adherence. This places additional onus on firms to implement access and security protocols like:

■ Strict data classification and protection schemes based on sensitivity
■ Access monitoring, access revocation processes, and auditing trails
■ Mandatory MFA for any remote access
■ Incident response and breach disclosure procedures
■ Appointing dedicated Data Protection Officers (DPOs)

Regulatory pressure has thus raised the levels of security standards in the alternative investment industry. However, stronger the security, the user access becomes more complex. Organizations need to create a fine line between locking data down and permission to use data in performing a job. Compliance and usability are not conflicting concepts but to cater to both the aspects it requires investment in security tools as well as user experience design.

8.4 Summary

In an alternative investment firm stakeholders could be in multiple geographies. While cloud computing and remote access technologies make the data available to authorized stakeholders in different parts of the world, the alternative investment firms need to ensure data safety. Ubiquitous secure access to systems allows alternative investment firms to realize productivity improvements, agility, and growth. A successful system access strategy should be based on an evaluation of operational needs and security requirements of the firm, and it requires constant re-evaluation making that strategy adaptable to evolution of technology and newer threats.

The chapter has examined the thin line which alternative investment managers should tread in provision of system access. The enterprise devices-versus-BYOD policies dilemma is not an either-or choice but a scale on which organizations have to find themselves based on specific requirements, culture, and risk tolerance level. When it comes to the security and accessibility of enterprise devices and BYOD, although enterprise devices may provide more control, BYOD can contribute to productivity improvement and employee contentment. Nevertheless, one solution does not fit all. Firms need to analyze their individual situations and determine which mix of policies, controls, and cultural factors will support their goals. The advancement of technology will bring changes to the ways of system access. Firms need to remain alive, flexible, and always aware of the trade-off between accessibility and security. Achieving a proper combination of accessibility and security is crucial.

Bibliography

Bitglass survey on BYOD adoption (www.helpnetsecurity.com/2020/
07/09/byod-adoption-is-growing-rapidly-but-security-is-lagging/).
CyberEdge's annual Cyberthreat Defense Report (CDR) 2022 (https://
cyber-edge.com/wp-content/uploads/2022/11/CyberEdge-2022-
CDR-Report.pdf).
CyberEdge's annual Cyberthreat Defense Report (CDR) 2023 (https://
cyber-edge.com/wp-content/uploads/2023/04/CyberEdge-2023-
CDR-Report-v1.0.pdf).
Microsoft Security's One simple action you can take to prevent
99.9 percent of attacks on your accounts (www.microsoft.com/
en-us/security/blog/2019/08/20/one-simple-action-you-can-take-
to-prevent-99-9-percent-of-account-attacks/).
Ponemon Institute's report on annual Cost of a Data Breach (www.
ibm.com/security/digital-assets/cost-data-breach-report/1Cost%20
of%20a%20Data%20Breach%20Report%202020.pdf).

Chapter 9

Technology Dilemma 6: How to Approach Technology Transformation?

9.1 Introduction

Alternative investment firms recognize the growing imperative to modernize systems, operations and automate processes through digital technologies. Transitioning from legacy platforms presents multifaceted challenges around developing strategy, migrating data, managing budgets, and driving adoption. Without thoughtful planning and execution, the complexity of transformation leads many initiatives to miss objectives and Return on Investment (ROI) targets. Firms need structured approaches to successfully evolve to more agile, insightful, and competitive technology environments.

                                   DOI: 10.1201/9781003481652-9

Previous chapters have looked at what to automate in an alternative investment firm, what services/solutions to choose, SaaS or on-premises deployments, perspective on automation cost versus value and fine balance between security and ease of access. Through these chapters, every stakeholder involved in the firm including the various business teams or IT team will be able to address the critical dilemmas around what needs to be achieved through technology in the context of their alternative investment needs. The remaining big questions which now must be addressed are: How to reach the desired target state? When that target state can realistically be achieved? What stays and what goes off? This chapter answers these questions and offers firms an approach to effectively reaching their target state.

This chapter provides a strategic framework to approach technology adoption and rollout specific to the alternative investment sector. It also explains how disciplines like enterprise architecture (EA) can help guide strategic roadmaps and system migrations. Organizational change management techniques are discussed to drive adoption across stakeholders. Recommendations aim to help firms maximize the value of technology investments while minimizing disruption through purposeful, phased modernization.

Each alternative investment firm is likely to have different current and target states defined for its IT systems. For that reason, each firm may need to develop a unique strategy and plan for effectively managing the transition from the current state to the target state based on guidelines, techniques, and best practices. This chapter also provides useful best practice guidelines for planning such a strategy.

9.2 Enterprise Architecture Helps or Not?

Any digital transformation will only be aspirational if not backed by a systematic process. True technology-driven evolution requires re-architecting systems, data, and operating models holistically based on strategic objectives. EA provides disciplines to tie modernization initiatives to business goals and formulate transition plans. EA can provide a structured framework and acts as the blueprint for systematically aligning IT strategy with business goals. According to Gartner, companies with a mature EA are twice as likely to meet their business outcomes.

This book doesn't intend to dive too deep into EA concepts, but it would be beneficial to briefly touch upon core components of EA:

- **Business Architecture**: Mapping business capabilities, processes, organizational structure, and revenue models. Identifies opportunities to improve operations and competitive positioning through technology.
- **Data Architecture**: Documents how data flows across systems, users, and applications. Facilitates building analytics, reporting, and data management strategy.
- **Application Architecture**: Catalogs existing software systems and relationships, overlaying suitability to desired future state. Defines consolidation, reuse, and gaps.
- **Technology Architecture**: Details hardware, infrastructure, and services enabling the technology ecosystem. Guides cloud, hosting, and platform strategies.
- **Security Architecture**: Frames controls, policies, access management, and other cyber risk mitigations needed to enable digital initiatives securely.

With current and future state architectures defined on all these pillars, the transformations needed to make the transition from one to the other can be identified. Gaps between the current and future state are indicators of technology investment or consolidation requirements. These gaps are planned to be plugged through process or technology changes and sequencing of these changes, that is, the roadmap evolves depending on the interdependencies. And since the needs are directly related to the business goals, thus modernization remains associated with real value rather than "bright shiny object" technologies.

The EA changes the way the organizations deal with the transformation, in a holistic, thoughtful, and measurable manner. The disciplines bring rigor that is often missing in technology initiatives. They also enable communication with business executives with the help of structured artifacts that represent the strategic direction. This creates credibility which is essential for funding and alignment.

Enterprise architecture (EA) is often seen as something for big organizations, and that it is an overkill for small- or mid-sized organizations. However, the EA disciplines can be useful for organizations of any size, but the degrees of formality and rigor to which they are implemented depend on the size and requirements of the organization. Here are some key considerations on applying EA in smaller firms:

- Even if the practices are informal, the core principles that are built on structured planning and alignment with business strategy are still beneficial to small firms.
- A reduced scale of EA can address the most critical domains only, that is, business architecture, data, and applications. Detail level might be lower.
- Visual artifacts such as capability maps, data flow diagrams and application interdependency diagrams assist in making decisions – firm size is immaterial.
- Even individual architects or consultants can apply EA tools and techniques on a project basis to ensure strategic alignment.
- Lightweight governance processes with senior leadership involvement might work better than excessive bureaucracy.

Making alternative investment firm users aware of the advantages of EA is a significant step but that's just the start. Next interesting challenge is to convince them with its applicability to their specific firm because just the use of the word "architecture" might sound complicated and overwhelming in an alternative investment firm. Table 9.1

Table 9.1 Common Challenges/Conflicts Encountered Related to "Architecture"

Challenges/Conflicts	Resolving Method/Argument
We are investment professionals – anything to do with "architecture" is a software architect's job. **Challenge:** Architecture, the word itself, seems too technical, formal, and engineering like.	Help business users understand that creating architecture is more about thinking holistically and determining what makes sense. It's not always technical as that would require using some tools or to be done by technology team only.
We are a private equity company, not an IT company; hence we need not follow typical software development cycle or a companywide architecture program. **Challenge:** Not recognizing that software development lifecycle and enterprise architecture are applicable to all firms.	If you have all the money in the world and you want to solve all your operational problems by spending more money, then yes you don't need enterprise architecture. But if you value opportunities to save operational costs by having a robust foundation or underlying structure, then architecture can definitely help.
There is already too much daily BAU (business as usual) stuff to do, so how can we find time for architecture tasks? **Challenge:** How to fit in system implementation tasks in people's diary?	As our funds grow in size, your daily work will increase anyway. Architecture work will reduce the growing pains of our business by ensuring decisions align to a long-term strategy.

Source: Author.

highlights some of such conflicts and arguments that business users may have.

Resolution methods/arguments suggested in Table 9.1 are aimed at emphasizing to the team members that a methodological "architecture" based approach is meant to provide a secure and scalable foundation that can adapt to their unique investment strategies and operational workflows in current as well as future times. If this challenge of convincing business users is also conquered, it will ensure that that people are aligned to the transformation program. On the whole, looking at technology projects holistically, assessing linkages, and keeping in line with business objectives is a generic best practice irrespective of firm size. EA does not require sophisticated artifacts or bureaucracy. Applied smartly, it can bring significant value to alternative investment firms of any size.

"Enterprise architecture is not just about IT; to be successful it must align the technology with business goals/strategy, ensuring every technology decision propels the organization forward", says Gareth Richardson, COO at Thought Machine.

9.3   Roadmap and Migration Planning

A well-defined roadmap and meticulous migration planning are vital to minimize disruptions during transformation. To be able to realistically plan for any transformation program there are two important steps:

- **Step 1:** Determine the logical sequencing of the incremental changes (the transition architectures).
- **Step 2:** Establish a set of business priorities within each change (or business prioritization).

These steps are discussed in detail later in this section; however, there are a few pre-requisites for any roadmap and migration plan:

- Consolidate requirements, solutions, and dependencies. For example, implementation of a new fund administration system can be done in parallel to the existing system, but its rollout will have a dependency on data from existing systems that will therefore need to be extracted, cleaned up, migrated, and tested on the new system.
- Identify any business drivers that might constrain the priority or sequence of implementation of IT projects. Assessment of the firm's culture and skills (both business and IT related) is also an important consideration as they could have an impact on the system transition and rollout decisions.
- Collate business risks and identify mitigations. Critical risks should be continuously monitored since they have the potential to disrupt the entire transformation project. For example, one of the risks while implementing a new investor reporting system could be that new compliance regulations (enforcing more transparency) might come into effect immediately after the system is ready.
- Decide which solution strategy and implementation methodology to use, as this will guide the transition architectures and implementation.

From a solution strategy perspective, stakeholders need to decide between a revolutionary or evolutionary approach. A revolutionary approach, for example, would mean switching off the current system completely and bringing in the new system to support the business processes of the firm. An evolutionary approach, on the other hand, is an approach of convergence; a parallel running or phased approach whereby new systems are introduced but co-exist with current systems for a defined duration. Systems that do not currently exist and which are going to be new implementations are categorized as a "greenfield" approach.

From an implementation methodology perspective, stakeholders need to decide the direction for implementation of the projects. One option could be to target quick wins first so that results are visible in the shorter term. This has the benefit of gaining the confidence of senior management regarding the overall transformation and it also helps to mitigate identified risks sooner. Another option could be to target high business value projects first, but this may be complex in nature and take longer to see real business benefits. The maturity of the alternative investment firm in terms of executing IT system projects also plays an important factor in deciding on the implementation methodology.

Stakeholders must discuss, evaluate, and agree on the solution strategy and implementation methodology since it becomes the basis of defining intermediate transition architectures. A transition architecture shows the firm at an architecturally significant state – that is between the existing state and the target state. Typically, business and technology drivers govern the number of steps and changes needed within each transition phase.

The common aim of all the technology and business drivers is to ensure that transition to the target architecture is more cost effective and operationally more efficient. Figure 9.1 shows a sample transition architecture diagram for an alternative investment firm which has minimal or no IT systems currently in place, but that wants to gradually embrace technology to enable and support core business functions. It presents a phase-wide view of the transition architecture highlighting what is achieved in different phases. Each phase involves detailed analysis and sequencing of transformation initiatives and requires best practices, such as establishing clear milestones, risk assessment, and involving stakeholders at every level.

Figure 9.2 illustrates the transition architecture from a different view – that is from an applications perspective. It

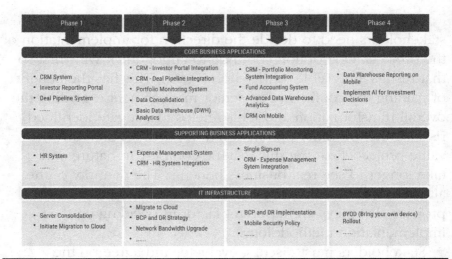

Figure 9.1 Sample Transition Architecture for an Alternative Investment Firm.

shows a sample transition architecture diagram for the deal pipeline, portfolio monitoring, and fund management systems for a private equity firm. In short, Figure 9.2 shows the lifecycle for different business applications and highlights in which phase an existing application would be decommissioned and new application is rolled out to support the corresponding business process.

In Figure 9.2, two examples are worth noting. First, the existing portfolio monitoring system would exist in stand-by mode during phase 2 (i.e., it will not be decommissioned, neither will it be actively used). However, if the new portfolio monitoring systems rollout runs into issues, then existing system could be brought back into action if required. By way of contrast, Figure 9.2 depicts an altogether different transition strategy – a parallel run – for a fund management system. In this case, both existing and new fund management systems will be operational during phase 3 (the new system will be rolled out, but all the transactions will have to be recorded in both

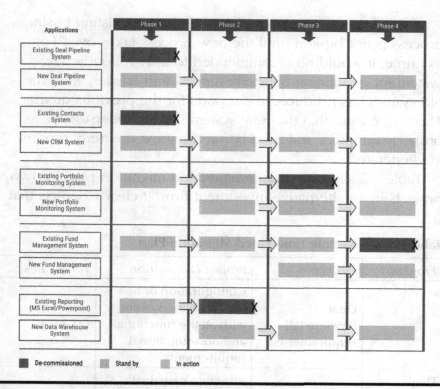

Figure 9.2 Sample Transition Architecture for an Alternative Investment Firm from Applications View.

existing and new systems). For the fund management team, this obviously means extra work, but the risk of accounting going wrong is largely mitigated since the original reference system is also up and running. A phased migration plan can allow an alternative investment firm to maintain 99.9% operational uptime.

It is worth noting that the duration/timeline of each phase is not a part of these transition architectures; those are handled in the migration planning. The review and approval of transition architectures confirms what needs to be achieved and the broad steps that need to be taken to reach the target state. The roadmap and migration plan stage determines what happens next and when.

A good migration plan will ensure that an existing business process is not broken until the new process takes over. For example, it would be recommended to only rollout a new system for generating quarterly reports immediately after the old system has produced the reports for the previous quarter. This will ensure that the new system is well understood, properly adopted, and used before the next quarterly reports are generated.

Table 9.2 shows a sample time-lined migration plan for two projects in an alternative investment firm. It clearly depicts that

Table 9.2   A Sample Time-Lined Migration Plan

Program	Project	Project Description	Timescales
Deal Pipeline	Deal Pipeline (all requirements)	Configuration of new deal pipeline system with all the functional and non-functional requirements	Q1 20XX
	Integration with CRM	Integrate new deal pipeline system with CRM system to enable flow of contact information mastered in CRM system	Q2 20XX
	...	...	...
CRM	CRM System (with all data migrated)	Setup of new CRM system with all data migrated from spreadsheets and old system	Q1 20XX
	CRM Web Services	Configure and expose webservices from CRM system so that other systems can integrate with it	Q1 20XX
	...	...	...

Source: Author

capabilities are built in logical steps and that the plan should reflect this. These timelines ensure the overall transformation phase, and its planning is concrete.

Chelsea Jin, MD & CFO Credit & Market at PAG, Hong Kong emphasizes, "Technology roadmap is like having a living plan that must adapt to both technological advancements and evolving business objectives. It clarifies objectives, aligns efforts, and defines the path forward".

9.4 Adoption Strategy within the Firm

One of the key components of implanting new technologies into day-to-day business operations is driving user adoption through change management. Organizational adoption is just as critical as technical deployment for a successful transformation. Adoption approach should not be a postscript; it needs to run parallel from the moment transformation is conceived of. It is therefore critical that the adoption strategy is comprehensive, taking into account the diversity of tech-savviness of the employees and stakeholders. The objective should be to reduce resistance, maximize effectiveness, and use the technologies to deliver on business goals. Employees need to adopt new ways of working and modifying business processes so as to utilize functionality. Leadership should also constantly re-echo the need and vision for change. Fostering adoption relies on four key elements:

- **Communications:** Continuous communication from executives on the objectives, timelines, expectations, and accomplishments of the transformation. Ensures understanding and acceptance at all levels.
- **Training and Support:** Hands-on training for users on new systems with continuous support materials. Enables people to utilize technologies effectively.

- **Incentives:** Recognizing teams and individuals for transformation progress. Could link to performance management.
- **Governance:** Leadership-driven steering committee overseeing the program to guide and align with business goals.

Transformation creates natural resistance if changes are forced down from above and without context. People require assistance in comprehending "what's in it for me" to fully adopt change. Placing activities around technology empowerment of people is appreciated. However, realistic expectations should be established as to timeframes, disruptions, and re-skilling. Constant request for the user's feedback allows subsequent enhancements to be adopted and process changes to be employed. Using power users as advocates and creating forums for input smooths transformation. Change management that is outstanding realizes the full potential of technology modernization.

The Technology Adoption Curve is a useful model for user adoption analysis. It identifies five user segments based on their propensity to adopt new technologies: Innovators, Early Adopters, Early Majority, Late Majority, and Laggards. Each of these groups has unique characteristics in the willingness and ability to accept change. Knowledge of these personas within the organization guides focused adoption plans. It is important to understand where different user groups and stakeholders of an organization are situated on the Technology Adoption Curve to create specific adoption plans. The approach should be individualized according to the specific points of view of each group. Focusing on their particular issues and motivations results in better adoption and tolerance of the new technologies in general.

A proven thought leader in change management, Chelsea Jin, highlights that "technology adoption doesn't just happen at the push of a button. It's a journey and is as much about people as it is about the technology itself".

9.5   Summary

Technological modernization offers alternative investment firms huge opportunities for growing and being more competitive. However, transformation paths are not without dangers of cost excesses, business interruption, and unfulfilled expectations if not dealt within a methodical way. A successful transformation is not just about technology, but also about people and processes. Therefore, transformation planning is one of the most important activities that should be managed and understood in context of an alternative investment firm's environment, risk appetite, business drivers, stuff landscape, and technology trends. It calls for holistic consideration of unique context of the firm and the dynamic nature of the alternative investment landscape.

The application of core disciplines, such as EA, roadmap prioritization, and change management, helps the firms in getting the maximum value from the technology investments and at the same time reducing execution risks. Based on these considerations the IT roadmap sequences the implementation of solutions to rectify identified gaps and overlaps in the IT architecture in line with business priority and timescales. A good plan should have adaptive capabilities to take care of dynamics that are bound to take place. It will ensure that the set of solutions is implemented properly and activate related support operations that will support the lifecycle of the implemented solution. Adoption strategy is also important for the successful incorporation of new technologies into daily activities. Therefore, technology transformation in the alternative investment sector is not a one-off project, but an ongoing process of enhancement and adjustment. In the famous words of Benjamin Franklin: "Failing to plan is planning to fail".

Chapter 10

Technology Trends Relevant to Alternative Investments Management

10.1 Introduction

The alternative investments industry has made technology a part and parcel of its operations, transforming the way that companies work and deliver value to investors. Adopting technology trends is not a matter of choice but a strategic necessity if the competitive advantage is expected to be sustained while managing complicated investment products. The alternative investment industry is at an inflection point where technology is a strategic asset more than an enabler. In the rapidly digitalizing world, firms get to use technology to create efficiency, improve returns, and satisfy demanding and sophisticated investors. This chapter touches on some of the current technology trends applicable to the alternative investment industry; technologies that not only address specific

                         DOI: 10.1201/9781003481652-10

operational business requirements but also add true value to the company.

10.2 Cloud Computing

Cloud computing is a transformative technology trend that alternative investment firms can exploit to improve operations, analysis, and market responsiveness. In the face of intensifying competition and changing economic landscapes, cloud-based systems with their agility and efficiency become the competitive advantage in comparison with reliance on legacy on-premises systems. Cloud solutions such as Amazon Web Services (AWS) and Microsoft Azure allow organizations to analyze large datasets and use innovative tools without significant investment in infrastructure. Cloud infrastructure and software delivery models adopting companies will be most ready to the future.

There are several compelling reasons alternative investment managers should make cloud migration a strategic priority:

- **Cost Efficiencies:** Cloud removes capital expenditures for on-premises data centers by moving to pay as you go operating expense models. This eliminates the idle capacity and increases the spending discretion. Automated management also reduces support costs.
- **Performance and Scalability:** Cloud-based system ensures easy access to the necessary computing power and storage, making it possible to handle complex risk models, what-if simulations, and the data-intensive workloads in a shorter period of time. Cloud infrastructure scales smoothly with growth.
- **Business Continuity:** Cloud is based on a world-class geographically dispersed data centers that use strong failover operation for high uptime and quick disaster recovery. This reduces operational risks.

- **Innovation:** Cloud providers can provide newer features faster through self-service interfaces. Firms have the ability to use AI, blockchain, quantum computing, and other emerging technologies without large inhouse investments.
- **Productivity:** Cloud-delivered software, workflows, and collaboration apps delivered via the cloud allow employees to be productive in any place. Desktop-as-a-service and virtual workspaces improve mobility.
- **Security:** Leading cloud providers come with very strong security controls and processes that are far beyond any capability that individual firms could achieve, including encryption, access controls, network security, and cyber threat monitoring.

Cloud options such as private clouds or government clouds give highly regulated alternative investment firms the flexibility of usage with additional data control and regionalization. Hybrid models are also an option to balance cloud benefits with sensitive on-premises systems.

Cloud computing is a trend for alternative investment management presenting paradigm shift due to scalability, resilience, and innovation of the technology. Cloud agility will be key in determining the winners and losers in an adaptive market environment under the pressure of fierce global competition. Properly architected and governed, alternative firms can migrate in an orderly fashion to cloud-based systems and data analytics that will form the future of investment management.

10.3 Artificial Intelligence and Machine Learning

Artificial intelligence (AI) encompasses a range of techniques to mimic human cognition, while machine learning (ML) is a specific subset of AI focused on algorithms that can improve and adapt based on experience. Much of what is branded as "AI" in finance builds on statistical and econometric modeling techniques that have existed for decades. The hype around AI and ML in some cases overstates the novelty of these technologies compared to proven quantitative methods. Having said that, AI and ML are at the forefront of predictive analytics and offer tremendous potential to enhance alternative investment strategies and operational processes. There are time-tested algorithms that can predict market trends and automate routine tasks, allowing investment professionals to focus on strategic decision-making. By detecting hidden predictive signals in market data, AI can surface new alpha opportunities and optimize portfolio composition based on risks, correlations, and statistical probabilities.

Primary ways AI and ML are transforming alternative investment management include:

- **Investment Research:** AI tools can facilitate the automation of the analysis of news, earnings reports, filings, research, and other sources of unstructured data to easily pull out the important insights without needing to read the whole material. Can also facilitate in analysis of vast amounts of market data aimed at identifying trends, patterns, and relationships which may indicate investment opportunities. This can bring into the light other factors and cues.

- **Investor Onboarding:** AI tools streamline repetitive manual processes, thus supporting faster and more customized investor onboarding and at the same time ensure compliance and security. Know Your Customer (KYC)/ Anti-Money Laundering (AML) processes can be automated through the use of Natural Language Processing (NLP) to extract required investor data from documents and forms. Compliance red flags can also be identified by ML models. Chatbots and virtual assistants are capable of answering routine onboarding questions and assisting investors with paperwork and requirements. This gives 24/7 self-service help. Technology can also monitor incoming wire transfers from investors and interface with banking systems to reconcile and confirm receipt of funds proactively.

- **Operational Efficiency:** By automating routine reporting, spreadsheet analysis, and data preparation these technologies allow analysts to focus on higher value judgments and strategy. AI tools can assist human analysts by creating custom visualizations, summaries, and performance attribution for the portfolios and underlying assets.

- **Portfolio Optimization:** AI tools can analyze correlations, scenario probabilities, and risk factors quickly across assets and thus suggest ideal portfolio balances that would deliver maximum projected returns within pre-defined risk limits. AI is able to predict volatility and risk exposure of different asset combinations in ML models that are trained on historical time series data. Sentiment analysis is also one of those fields where AI can offer a lot.

- **Compliance:** AI can automate KYC/AML screening of investors and counterparties by using NLP to extract entities from documents and check against the sanctions lists. Tools are able to analyze e-mails, communications, and other records to identify regulatory risks, anti-competitive practices, or breaches of codes of conduct. Time-tested algorithms of anomaly detection may be used with transaction records to detect likely occurrences of fraud or money laundering. Tools can continuously monitor for cyber threats, vulnerabilities, and abnormal access patterns that could lead to compromised investor data. Significant manual effort can be saved by automating generation of compliance reports for regulations.

- **ESG Monitoring:** AI technology can analyze unstructured data like earnings calls, news, and filings to automatically score companies on ESG metrics based on mentions of relevant terms. It can process sustainability reports and other disclosures to check company ESG claims against published data and standards. It can also help in optimizing ESG-integrated portfolio construction constrained by risk, return and ESG score thresholds. Technology can automate ESG reporting for investors and regulators to provide transparency into sustainability objectives.

10.4 Blockchain

Blockchain, the groundbreaking digital ledger underpinning cryptocurrencies, is transforming the alternative investments industry. This decentralized recordkeeping technology provides unparalleled security, transparency, and efficiency. Beyond its origins in digital currencies, blockchain brings immense possibilities for reshaping alternative investments. Blockchain distributes data over the networks and optimizes transactions which makes blockchain an answer to many challenges of alternative investments.

The ledger, which is tamperproof and unchangeable, at the heart of the blockchain technology, introduces incomparable transparency and trustworthiness to alternative investments. Each transaction in a blockchain is time stamped and strung along open chronological ledger. This allows all involved parties to have full access to the identical confirmable information and minimizes risk for fraud or fake reporting. Real estate investments are a meaningful example of the benefits of blockchain. The technology can provide an unquestionable, timeless record of ownership, valuations, and transactions on a property. This kind of transparency builds trust and confidence with the investors as it shortens due diligence process of the required information, which can be accessed and authenticated on the blockchain.

Due diligence for alternative investments is usually a complicated and lengthy process, requiring a variety of asset and background verifications. One of the advantages of blockchain technology is that it can significantly simplify due diligence, acting as single and indisputable truth. As blockchain ledgers are immutable and globally available, investors could quickly validate asset histories and authenticity without long audit processes. The transparency drastically reduces the due diligence process that in turn allows faster decisions and transactions. Blockchain can keep clean records of the financial transactions, shareholder agreements, and performance metrics of a company for private equity investments. This data being stored on the blockchain facilitates due diligence for potential investors and speeds up the investment cycle. Overall, blockchain streamlines due diligence through immutable, shared records, allowing alternative investors to vet opportunities and act faster.

10.5   Business Continuity Planning

Business continuity planning (BCP) is especially vital in the high-stakes alternative investments arena, which involves substantial capital outlays and investor anticipations. This sector, covering hedge funds, private equity, real estate, and commodities, frequently handles elaborate, illiquid assets and leans heavily on market steadiness and investor trust. Any operational disruption can rapidly escalate into significant financial and reputational damage. BCP is critical, especially evidenced during the COVID-19 pandemic. During COVID-19, technologies supported BCP efforts, such as remote desktop protocols, virtual private networks (VPNs) and cloud-based collaboration tools, ensuring firms remain operational during disruptions.

Increased regulations and investor scrutiny require alternative investment firms to have robust BCP practices in place. The UK's Financial Conduct Authority (FCA) Handbook in section SYSC 3.2.19 says:

> A firm should have in place appropriate arrangements, having regard to the nature, scale and complexity of its business, to ensure that it can continue to function and meet its regulatory obligations in the event of an unforeseen interruption. These arrangements should be regularly updated and tested to ensure their effectiveness.

Similarly, in the United States, the Securities and Exchange Commission (SEC), says in Rule 206(4)-4:

> The proposed rule would require SEC-registered advisers to adopt and implement written business continuity and transition plans reasonably designed to address operational and other risks related to a significant disruption in the investment adviser's operations.

Growth of technology also increases cyber risks thus necessitating plans for data, hardware, and software recovery after an attack. Remote working poses additional BCP challenges for alternative investment firms.

Technology has transformed how BCP is done. Alternative investment firms are moving toward cloud-based solutions as they offer scalable, flexible, and cost-effective options for data storage and backup. Remote access to systems and data has also become easy with cloud computing. Cybersecurity is a critical component of BCP, and alternative investment firms are adopting advanced security measures like multi-factor authentication, end-to-end encryption, and continuous monitoring to protect sensitive data and systems.

10.6 Mobility

Mobiles have become the most common tools used to access information. With an increasing need for on-the-go access to data and systems, mobility solutions are vital. Mobile phones and pads are finding their way into enterprises and their adoption is on meteoric rise. The use of such devices in an alternative investment firm can be broadly classified into three categories: secure access to email; secure access to documents and secure access to enterprise applications/data. Enhanced mobility enables alternative investment firms to adopt flexible and remote working arrangements. This improves business continuity capabilities and productivity. Mobile access to critical systems and data via tablets/smartphones allows for real-time information and quicker decision making by investment professionals when on-the-go or working remotely.

Mobility solutions hold the potential to optimize numerous processes for alternative investment firms, spanning from due diligence and deal completion to portfolio administration and reporting. Remote accessibility and digital workflows brought about by mobility introduce efficiencies that reduce costs and enhance the overall returns of investment holdings. Alternative investment professionals can conduct onsite due diligence, review deals, approve transactions, and manage assets in real time through mobile platforms, regardless of their location. For instance, a real estate-focused alternative investment firm can leverage mobile augmented reality (AR) technology in improving the due diligence process. Technology allows investors to conduct virtual property tours, access real-time data on property performance, and visualize future developments. This seamless coordination leads to quicker and more informed investment decisions. Mobility also allows for 24/7 digital reporting and portfolio analytics, providing real time performance insights to investors at any time. Investor portals and mobile apps enable investors to have continuous access to their alternative investment account data and fund information from anywhere. The result is that alternative investment firms stand to make significant cost savings and increased productivity that reflects on the profitability of their funds, as they adopt mobile capabilities. Ultimately, mobility delivers the tools and connectivity for alternative investors to maximize their agility, insight, and value creation across the investment lifecycle.

10.7 Enterprise Search

Alternative investments being an information-rich industry, the ability to quickly find and retrieve data is key. Enterprise Search technology refers to the capability of making content from multiple enterprise-type sources (like databases, intranets, file systems, software applications, document management systems, and emails) easily searchable by users.

The alternative investment sector is witnessing significant advancements in Enterprise Search technology. AI and ML allow Enterprise Search tools to deliver more precise and contextual results through enhanced search accuracy, relevance, and personalization. AI and ML power semantic search capabilities that understand user intent. NLP enables intuitive, user-friendly search by allowing free-form queries in plain language instead of requiring specific keywords. This greatly benefits alternative investors in finding specialized investment information. Predictive analytics and search functionalities utilize AI to anticipate user needs proactively and surface insightful trends to guide strategic choices.

Enterprise Search solutions are increasingly capable of integrating and aggregating data from a wide range of sources, including cloud-based services, internal databases, and third-party platforms. This is a very critical need especially if an alternative investment firm chooses to go with different service providers for automating different parts of their operations. This ensures comprehensive search results and supports better-informed investment decisions.

As cybersecurity threats evolve, so do the security features of Enterprise Search tools. Search tools deploy advanced security and privacy controls such as encryption, access restrictions, and privacy features to keep sensitive investment data protected while still searchable as cyber threats advance. Some of the established search tools are Elastisearch, Apache Solr, Algolia, Amazon CloudSearch, and Microsoft Azure Cognitive Search.

10.8   Business Intelligence and Analytics

Business intelligence (BI) is a set of applications and processes that transform business raw data into meaningful and useful information. BI is not about just having the data but more importantly about having the capability to collate and analyze the data to derive actionable insights, influencing decision-making processes and strategic directions.

For an alternative investment firm, it is critical to be able to draw comparisons and conduct analysis on desirable parameters when looking at the deal pipeline, portfolio companies or fund data. It is equally important to be able to analyze and have a forward-looking view of investment performance by tweaking certain parameters that can change over time (e.g., the portfolio's financial data and currency fluctuations). This is the power that a BI and analytics technology platform can provide enabling investment analysts to effectively use their time in actual data analysis rather than pulling, collating, and generating graphs every time.

BI and analytics tools are also embracing technology trends to make their systems even more effective. With time majority of these platforms now offer cloud-based BI services and are becoming more popular due to obvious benefits like scalability, cost-effectiveness, and ability to manage large datasets. They have capabilities of text and speech analytics extracting insights from unstructured data like news, research reports, earnings calls and more. Some tools can also help in sentiment analysis of market chatter and social media supporting timely evaluation of investment narratives. AI capabilities are automating complex analytical processes for rapid insights and recommendations.

Some of the alternative investment software providers offer in-built BI capabilities but that is restricted to the data which those applications process. To have an enterprise-wide BI capability other technology products may need to be considered such as Tableau, Power BI, QlikView, AWS Quick Sight, and iLevel, among others. Overall, BI and analytics are becoming critical for alternative investors to capitalize on data-driven insights for improved asset allocation, risk management, and investment performance.

10.9   Virtual Data Rooms

To put it simply, a virtual data room (VDR) is a technology solution that allows online document sharing; a repository of information used for both storing and distributing documents only to the intended audience. VDRs have been essential for secure document sharing during fundraising, due diligence, and audit processes. VDRs have been there for a while however early VDRs primarily offered basic document storage and viewing capabilities. Security features were often basic, focusing mainly on access controls and password protection. The user interface and experience were not as streamlined, or intuitive and collaboration features were also less sophisticated. There was limited integration with other business tools, and mobile access was not as advanced or widespread.

Over the last 10 years or so VDRs have evolved a lot. Today, they include advanced encryption, multi-factor authentication, watermarking, and detailed user activity tracking. User experience is hugely enhanced, and these tools now offer integration with a range of business tools and platforms, including CRM systems, project management tools, and communication platforms. VDRs now include features that help firms comply with global data protection regulations like GDPR. Solutions are also more tailored to the specific needs of alternative investment sector, including features designed for private equity, venture capital, real estate, and hedge funds.

There are many VDR technology solution providers (e.g., Datasite, Intralinks, DealRoom, and iDeals) in the market catering specifically to private equity, venture capital, and similar industry domains.

10.10   Zero Trust Security

Zero Trust security has emerged from a concept to an imperative model for the alternative investment sector, known for high-value transactions and sensitive data. This approach eliminates implicit trust by continuously validating every access attempt. The mantra of "never trust, always verify" underscores Zero Trust's principles amid intensifying cyber threats, remote work, and cloud adoption.

Within alternative investment firms, Zero Trust policies ensure only authorized users and devices can access resources after authentication. Protecting confidential investment data and client information is accomplished by applying Zero

Trust to data usage. Adopting Zero Trust also aids regulatory compliance.

Adopting Zero Trust strengthens the organization against cyberattacks, which in turn minimizes the risks of data breaches and insider threats. Streamlining of security operations in automated verification enhances efficiency. Zero Trust implemented as a strong security measure is considered a strong policy, which ensures investor confidence in terms of the protection of assets and information. Nonetheless, integration, training, and resource challenges should be sorted out.

Zero Trust security is crucial for alternative investment because it protects assets, maintains compliance, and enhances trust. Its future evolution is set to reshape cybersecurity landscape as threats remain. Zero Trust, which is based on strong identity and access controls, allows alternative investment firms to secure their most important systems and data.

10.11 Investor Communications

Clear and consistent investor relations and reporting is vital for alternative investment firms to maintain trust, transparency, and satisfaction. Investors want regular updates on portfolio performance, risk exposures, capital flows, and other metrics to make informed decisions. There are several technology trends that are helping alternative investment firms make effective and efficient investor communication ensuring investors stay informed and engaged.

Investor portals provide a centralized space for sharing documents, reports, and updates with investors. These platforms allow investors access information anytime, anywhere and with security features like fine-grained access control, encryption and multi-factor authentication establishes trust and confidence.

Investors expected alternative investment firms to adhere to standardized reporting. The implementation of standards like Institutional Limited Partners Association (ILPA) principles has profoundly transformed investor communications within alternative investments. These guidelines have driven greater transparency, consistency, and efficiency in interactions between general partners (GPs) and limited partners (LPs). When selecting a software, it's a very important criteria to check on if compliant reports are supported by the platform.

Automated and personalized communication with investors using tools like CRM (e.g., Salesforce) is on the rise. While emails remain an important pillar in investor communication but having a tool streamlines this process and ensures consistent connection. AI and data analytics enable personalized communication, tailoring messages and reports to individual investor preferences and behaviors.

Looking ahead, investor communications in alternative investments may evolve toward a more unified omnichannel approach. This will enable alternative investment managers to engage with investors through a steady, seamless experience across platforms.

10.12 Paperless Compliances

The alternative investment industry is heavily regulated and document intensive. However, emerging technologies are enabling funds to transition many compliance processes to paperless digital workflows, driving higher efficiency, accuracy, and sustainability. Regulations have also changed and now favor or require timely digital reporting and compliance mechanisms. Globally there is a shift toward sustainability and reduce of paper use and technological innovation is supporting paperless environment. Paperless compliances streamline the compliance processes and leads to cost and time savings. With digital documents and compliance records security measures can also be enhanced as necessary. Auditing is also easy as all the communication is digital and transparent.

Alternative investment firms are implementing cloud-based systems with document management capabilities. For investor onboarding automated workflows are increasingly becoming popular integrated with data rooms or investor portal for data sharing. AI tools are being used to review submitted compliance documents and raise alerts. For asset verification, blockchain-based systems are being adopted.

Transitioning compliance processes to digital mode is a rising imperative for alternative investment firms to gain efficiency, security, and cost benefits while meeting regulatory expectations. Eliminating paper lays the groundwork for more innovation in compliance as emerging technologies proliferate.

10.13   Summary

Through various trends this chapter has reiterated the importance of technology in alternative investments management. There is every possibility that by the time this book is published there may be a few additions to the list of technology trends listed in this chapter; such is the pace of technology evolution these days. The objective here is not to present a comprehensive list but to inform alternative investment firms about what is potentially available to them, so they are better prepared to keep an eye on and adopt upcoming technology trends. And it is not only the IT executives but also business users in alternative investment firms who will increasingly need to be more equipped to keep up with the pace of technology innovation.

Although technology delivers a competitive advantage, alternative investment firms must carefully implement it in line with their specific business aims and investment approaches. Effective technology integration requires strategic and thoughtful planning to maximize value and benefits.

In summary, technology stands as a foundational pillar of the future of alternative investment management. Adopting technology solutions can yield immense benefits, but organizations must thoughtfully map technology rollouts onto wider business goals to realize the full potential. The most thriving alternative investment firms will be distinguished not only by their savvy use of technologies, but also by an organizational culture encouraging ongoing innovation and education.

With a deliberate strategy guiding technology deployment, alternative investment managers can transform operations, decision-making, and customer experiences. However, technology for its own sake rarely succeeds without alignment to business objectives and investor needs. Alternative firms must look inward at their unique vision and processes before looking outward at technology capabilities. With planning and vision, alternative investment managers can leverage technology as a catalyzing force to propel sustainable growth and value creation.

Bibliography

Financial Conduct Authority (FCA) Handbook – a collection of the FCA's legal instruments and other provisions (www.handbook.fca.org.uk/handbook/SYSC/)
Securities and Exchange Commission's ruling on Business Continuity and Transition Plans (www.sec.gov/files/rules/proposed/2016/ia-4439.pdf)

Index